CLOTHE
YOUR SPIRIT

CLOTHE YOUR SPIRIT

Dressing for Self-Expression

JENNIFER ROBIN

Spirit Press, San Francisco

Library of Congress Cataloguing-in-Publication Data

Robin, Jennifer, 1956-
    Clothe Your Spirit.

    1. Clothing and dress.   2. Beauty, Personal.
I. Title.
TT507.R63 1987   646'.34   87-23494
ISBN 0-944296-03-3

Design and production by Jaeger & Associates.
Author photo by Jay Daniel
Back cover photo by Ronald J. Carter
All other photos by Jennifer Robin

Manufactured in the United States of America.

For all the love . . .
and all the support . . .

To My Husband
Jerry Freeman

Table of Contents

Author's Note

The photographs in this book started out simply as a record of my work as an image consultant. When I shopped with my clients for new clothes, the day flew buy in a flurry of shopping bags and cash transactions. I hated for it all to be over without a chance to reflect on the glory of the finished product. I wanted to capture the moment, and also allow my client to fully experience the impact of the transformation. When "Clothe Your Spirit" became a book ready for publication, I considered having the photographs of my subjects professionally redone. I finally decided there was an authenticity to my amateur attempts that a studio setting would be unable to duplicate. The moment when my client first experienced wearing her new clothes could never be recaptured.

In the Spring of 1987, two years after many of the earlier photos were taken, I visited a number of my original subjects. As I updated their photographs, it was clear that both an inner and outer evolution had taken place. The faces that smiled back at me reflected an ease and comfort that obviously originated from within. The changes that had taken place in the lives of Debbie, Holly, Gloria, and Serita were the most compelling. The stories and comments I have excerpted throughout the book allow the reader to follow these diverse women through the Clothe Your Spirit process.

Even though no men are featured in this book, Clothe Your Spirit is not an approach exclusively for women. I also work with men who enjoy the benefits of dressing for self-expression. I have noticed, however, that the needs of men and women are different; women have a more difficult time developing a realistic or positive body image, while men suffer more from lack of experience and self-confidence in clothes selection. This book is written to address the special concerns of women, to work through their fears about "measuring up" and to break down the barriers that prevent them from seeing themselves more clearly. The specific focus on women is not to suggest that Clothing Your Spirit is any less important for men—everyone can benefit from expressing their uniqueness more fully.

INTRODUCTION

Clothe Your Spirit: An Outward Celebration of Your Uniqueness

There is more than one way to approach the goal of looking great. The traditional methods—sculpting your body into a vision of toned perfection, coloring your hair, changing your nose, and doing all you can to retard the process of aging—are not the only approach. You can try another approach, one that stresses self-expression over self-improvement. Clothe Your Spirit is a process of redirecting the energy that has gone into perfecting your exterior toward developing an awareness and appreciation of your individuality. You will achieve the desired result of looking great, but you will accomplish it in a different way, through a process of personal discovery. Clothe Your Spirit is an adventure that will transform your relationship with your wardrobe and, in turn, with yourself.

We care so much about our clothing because, in addition to it helping us look our best, it tells people something about us. We know that clothing does more than protect our bodies from the elements and our decency from probing eyes. Whether we like it or not, clothing communicates. With this tool at our disposal, the question becomes, "What do we want to communicate?"

The desire for others to see us as we really are, to recognize our spirit, is one of the most powerful emotions we experience in our dealings with others. When I meet someone, I want them to see *me*—the individual, the unique combination of qualities that I have developed and nurtured for my thirty-odd years on this planet. I want others to recognize the specialness that I feel about myself. I want the people I come into contact with to discover that I am warm, loving, fun, and interesting—the qualities of a good friend or colleague. I want them to know that I am straightforward and direct, yet wise and thoughtful; creative and artistic, with a flair for the dramatic. I am also delicate and strong, sensual and womanly.

The expressive quality of my face, my smile, the sparkle in my eyes, and the way I move say a lot about the kind of person I am. The other form of immediate visual communication is how I am dressed. It takes time to know the true essence of a person, so we rely on our visual impressions to help us. If we like what we see, a spark ignites, and we are curious to fan the flames by knowing more.

Clothes make the introductions and break the ice, whether we are in line at the neighborhood deli or across a conference table. If you ask yourself what you want your clothes to say to others, you know in your heart that you want them to say far more than chic, stylish, rich, or successful. Others want to know what is special about you too, not how well you can emulate the current fashion ideal.

Clothe Your Spirit is a process of learning to make your outward communication exactly what you want it to be. It begins with the realization that you were created a package deal, inside and out. Recognizing that your spirit seeks expression in your physical presentation can shift your entire focus of wardrobing.

It is understandable that you would not want to identify with anything you feel is "flawed," especially when our culture says that to look perfect is to be perfect. Liking yourself does not mean you dismiss any desire for improvement. But putting all your energy into changing or camouflaging your "flaws" is not nearly as effective in bringing about the results you want as concentrating on the aspects of yourself that you like.

Looking beautiful is having the confidence to act as if you are. How you perceive yourself has everything to do with how you look. The people whose appearance you admire believe they have assets worth flattering. Did you ever consider that the appeal of slenderness is based not on the inherent beauty of slim bodies, but on the permission granted to the owners to like themselves? Imagine that the exact shape of your body was currently the most sought after and desirable form. Wouldn't you proudly show it off? The Clothe Your Spirit process of discovering your remarkable qualities will teach you to make the most of them. You already admire aspects of yourself, from the shape of your face to the strength of your character, and bringing attention to these points will start a chain reaction of further positive revelations.

It takes a conscious effort to make the most of your assets, because, unless you happen to be five feet ten inches tall and classically gorgeous, they may not be readily apparent to you. Our culture has a ridiculously limited ideal of what constitutes physical perfection: tall, thin, and young. Being blond doesn't hurt, high cheekbones are always nice, and long legs and a flat stomach are a given. The current limited attitude about what constitutes physical beauty has left everyone else with the impression that they are somehow lacking. Not thin enough, not beautiful enough, not rich enough, and not clever enough. This feeling is so ingrained that most of us never question its validity. We just do our best to conform and dislike ourselves when we can't. For a nation that prides itself on its diversity, on being a so-called "melting pot," we have the most limited respect for physical uniqueness in the world. We do not appreciate the roundness of curvy, solidly built women, or the delicacy of small, slender men. In our society, there is only one, "perfect" way to look.

Curiously enough, we do recognize that it takes all kinds of people to make this world an interesting place. Who would deny that we need a blend of skills and talents, a balance of opposing points of view? Our society depends upon the designs of creative minds and the strong bodies that carry them out. How dull life would seem without the differences among skilled craftsmen, quiet scholars, and animated performers—not just for the variety of tasks performed, but for the marvelous diversity of spirit.

Saying we should all aspire to one ideal of physical perfection is about as exciting as wishing for a nation populated only by lawyers—or image consultants, for that matter. Yet I cannot deny that the feelings to "measure up" are powerful ones. Unfortunately, believing you are inferior dooms your chances of creating a wardrobe you can be happy with. A sense of personal inadequacy is at the root of many clothes-buying woes. Disliking the clothes you buy, never having the right thing to wear, overspending, and feeling unattractive and untalented, are all part of the same problem—lack of definition and appreciation of your uniqueness.

If you are like most women, you feel if you lost weight you would look better, and if you looked better you would like yourself more. We spend vast amounts of precious mental and physical energy in a quest for the perfect figure, trying to fit the mold. "Just a few more pounds," you promise yourself, and then you will be okay. Then you will be able to go shopping and buy something you really love, something that looks great on you.

Ironically, those of you who have succeeded in losing weight and achieving a physical appearance that you thought would satisfy you have discovered (much to your surprise) that you don't necessarily feel good about your ability to create a wonderful wardrobe. "How could that be?" you wonder in amazement, "I did what I thought would make it all better." The same pressure that motivated you to sculpt your body is still there, but there is nothing to help you celebrate yourself once you have arrived at the pearly gates of slenderdom.

Slenderness is not the magic key that unlocks all doors. As a wardrobe consultant, I see that confusion comes in all shapes and sizes. You might approve of yourself more when you are thinner, but when I work with clients their size has little to do with how beautiful they will ultimately look and feel. I don't have a preference for size 4's over 14's. Everyone has a spirit that shines and assets to be brought forth. My challenge, and yours, is to discover them.

Accepting my assertion does not mean an immediate end to all self-criticism. If only it were that simple! Learning to like yourself as you are is part of the Clothe Your Spirit process. You do not need to take yourself in hand and try to jack up your confidence and self-esteem in order to begin. The way out of the need to constantly "measure up" is to understand that self-expression is an acknowledgment of where you are at the moment. Expression has no judgments, no right or wrong, no good or bad. Your spirit is there waiting to be revealed. Wherever you are now is the perfect place to begin.

How we feel about ourselves is so much a part of how we look that the two must overlap and support each other. You cannot reach your full beauty potential without completely approving of yourself; neither can you like your appearance more just by wishing it were so. Seeing yourself in stunning new clothing that expresses your spirit and flatters your assets will help you see your most attractive self.

Buying clothes and creating a wardrobe you love can be a real pleasure, but for many the joy is missing. Clothe Your Spirit is designed to help you enjoy wardrobe planning, because when a project is fun and allows you to feel good about yourself, it will be more successful. Looking at clothes as a vehicle to express your inner nature provides an exciting new twist. It may seem a bit farfetched now to imagine holding up a garment and asking yourself, "Does this express my personality?" but you will see that clothing can convey far more than you ever dreamed possible.

Clothe Your Spirit will serve as a guidebook for your journey into uncharted personal territory. It will help you to examine your beliefs past and present, to look at your needs today, and to actively create your dream for the future. This book is divided into three sections: "Breaking Down Barriers"; "Discovering Your Uniqueness"; and "Planning and Implementing Your Ideal Wardrobe." The first step in the Clothe Your Spirit process is to break down some of the barriers that stand in the way of your success. You cannot make the most of your good qualities if something or someone has convinced you that you have no assets worth flattering. Barriers are in your way before you ever set foot in a store. Even if you know what you like and have a feel for what looks good on you, doubting your worthiness will hold you back from the full expression of your spirit. Acknowledge those nagging, critical feelings as the full-blown stumbling blocks they really are. When you recognize a negative attitude, you then have the opportunity to evaluate its validity and, if necessary, change it.

The next step in the process is to look at your spirit and its relationship to your physical being. The second section offers a useful technique that helps you identify your spirit in terms that relate to fashion. You will then embark on a search for your assets with my personal assurance that every person has at least five.

Getting ready to put together a new wardrobe requires advance planning, which includes a careful examination of your lifestyle, a thorough survey of your closet, and some creative exploration of the way you would ultimately like to look. The third section of the book provides exercises that will help you produce the results you want. A certain amount of reflection is important and necessary, but Clothe Your Spirit involves as much "doing" as it does thinking. Action produces change. Before you venture into the stores, you will be armed with pertinent information plus a plan to avoid the nasty zombies that lurk in dressing rooms. When you follow this approach, your shopping trips will be different.

In addition to absorbing the upcoming advice and information, there is something very important you must to do. During the process of Clothing Your Spirit, you need to treat yourself as kindly as possible. In my work I must get close enough to someone to discover her spirit and take a good look at who she is. If someone is brave enough to expose herself to me, I must win her trust. I therefore never criticize or speak harshly or cruelly. Honesty is tempered with kindness. I am always aware of people's sensitive, vulnerable natures, and if I touch a nerve, I back off. I treat people this way not only because I am a nice person; I do it because it works.

You must take this same approach with yourself. During this process you must be as patient, kind, accepting, and loving as you possibly can. Harping on your flawed body, your wrinkles, or your past shopping mistakes does not work. Being negative, harsh, or critical will only drive you farther away from yourself.

Gentle handling is magical. It will heal the scars of childhood taunts, rude remarks, and hundreds of nightmarish trips to the dressing room. It will allow your delicate spirit to come forward. As you accept it, your spirit will grow confident and flourish.

When you start to believe in yourself, a powerful tool will come to your aid. It sharpens with practice and use, until it becomes honed to precision—the feeling you have deep down inside, the unequivocal knower of truth, *your own voice of intuition and inner affirmation.* Your intuitive reactions are your best ally when you are shopping, cleaning your closet, or deciding what to wear. With awareness, attention, and practice, they will become loud, clear, and definite. They will tell you when you have presented on the outside the essence of who you are on the inside.

An increased awareness of who you are is developing all the time. The spirit you begin to clothe now will be different a year from now. The process of living does more than create sags and wrinkles. Would any of us really trade what we have learned for firmer flesh and fewer grey hairs? How you grow and change, and what you learn about yourself, is an ongoing part of Clothing Your Spirit. As our spirit changes throughout our lifetime, what we want to communicate grows and changes along with it. You do not feel the same at forty as you did at eighteen, and you do not want to dress in the same way either. You may miss that firmer, more youthful body, but you would never trade it for the wisdom and experience you now possess.

The subtle growth of our confidence over time often goes unnoticed. How easy it is to recall an idealized vision of what we were like during our younger days. We were fresher, lovelier; we stood taller. In our rose-tinged fantasy, we forget the self-consciousness, the doubts, the aching need for peer approval that went along with it. It is exciting to realize that the experiences of living and learning can improve our appearance. Instead of fearing that your assets will disappear, imagine them growing clearer, sharper, more well defined every year. As you look at the evolution of the photographs of the women in this book, notice how an awareness of their spirit and their assets has enhanced their appearance.

Clothing is an unmined resource for expressing and experiencing personal growth. As you begin to think about clothing as an expression of who you are, you start the process of inner reflection and the changes that are inevitable. When you concentrate on specifics, finding clothes that look wonderful on you, that fit exactly the needs of your lifestyle and constraints of your budget, will become an exciting challenge. No mountaintop meditation is involved in this experience of self-discovery.

The Clothe Your Spirit approach does not require that you suspend all your previous beliefs. Try the suggestions that sound as if they might work for you.

Your personal involvement in the project is what brings the ideas to life. Handling yourself gently and tuning in to your intuitive reactions allow you to choose what works for you. Trying something new and seeing it result in a positive change will stimulate other areas to develop and grow.

Liking yourself in an ivory tower is one thing, but feeling happy and comfortable about the way you present yourself to the world is another. You need to see results, and Clothing Your Spirit will help you see those results. Regardless of the whims or trends of fashion, you will be guided by an awareness of your spirit, a belief in your own inner voice, and an ability to decide what is right for you. Each new season's styles will no longer seem like a mandate, a necessity for being "in," but rather they will be options for you to choose from. When you are dressed to express the best of who you are, you can forget yourself and your appearance and enjoy the beauty of the world around you.

Before you can begin to discover your spirit, your assets, and your unique style, a few walls have to come a-tumbling down. If you are ready for a change, then let's get started.

PART ONE

Breaking Down Barriers

1

Weight and Body Image

You probably believe that there is "a good reason" why you have been unable to achieve the look that you would like from your clothing. Some people are convinced that they weigh too much to fit into current styles, others perceive a shortage of cash, while still others doubt their attractiveness. Before we begin the actual steps that lead to discovering how your spirit relates to clothing, it is important to recognize the beliefs and barriers that stand in the way of you accomplishing your goals. Unless you take the time to consider your own personal stumbling blocks, you will find yourself coming up with excuses why Clothe Your Spirit will not work for you.

Last spring I bought a wonderful new dress. When I tried it on, I stood in front of the dressing room mirror and said to myself, "This dress is perfect. I look absolutely wonderful in it. It couldn't look any better. In fact, I don't need to lose even one pound to improve it." When I got home, I couldn't believe it was true, so I tried it on again. Twisting and craning to check the mirror for any previously unnoticed offenses, I concluded that losing weight would not improve my appearance at all.

Six months later my new dress was too big.

The simple act of liking yourself, without qualifications, has an amazingly powerful effect. The good feelings I had about myself did not spur me on to yet another diet. In fact, quite the opposite was true. The fight to create a more perfect body went out of me. That nasty little voice with the unrelenting message "You're not good enough," had stilled, easing the lingering unhappiness that had been a part of my life since I was fifteen years old. A tranquil acceptance subtly took its place. I did not need to convince myself that I looked good; I saw for myself that I did. I found it was much easier to eat in harmony with my body's needs, and the remaining pounds that plagued me gradually slipped away.

Many of my clients have also experienced gradual weight losses as a result of clothing their spirits. They may not be as slender as they had always dreamed, but their weight has stabilized at a place that is appropriate and comfortable for them. When I get together with clients after not seeing them for several months, I often notice that their clothes look looser and roomier. When I question them they invariably reply, "I don't know how it happened exactly, but it seems easier not to eat as much."

If you are puzzled and unhappy about never being able to lose weight permanently, concentrating on Clothing Your Spirit will help. When the harsh, critical taskmaster is at the helm, losing weight becomes a battle shrouded in unclear frustration. It probably does not make sense to you that something you strive for so actively and want so badly is so achingly unobtainable.

Clothe Your Spirit is not a weight-loss program, yet sometimes a physical transformation is part of the process. Reaching the point where I could naturally lose weight was slow in coming. It took time to see beyond my flaws, to discover my assets, and to learn to see myself realistically as a whole person. I experimented with clothes, and shopped even when I was afraid I might be terribly disappointed. Eventually, I started to appreciate things about myself, and was able to choose clothes that truly flattered my face and body.

The secret of looking wonderful *is* making the most of your assets. I saw it for myself that day in the dressing room. I still thought I weighed ten pounds too much, but there I was, looking terrific. What was so spectacular about this dress? The sophisticated, sensuous lines were well suited to my spirit and the style was perfect for my figure. The soft jersey fabric fell straight from my shoulders to my hips and gathered with a wide, fanny-wrap. The wrap was low enough to draw attention away from my short waist and the fabric draped gracefully, camouflaging my tummy. My breasts and hips gave shape to the silhouette. Finally, the knee-length hem and push-up sleeves showed off my shapely arms and legs.

Oh, the joy of something that fits just right! When you have a flattering, comfortable outfit on, you feel good all over. A garment fitting perfectly does not depend upon being slender; it requires an exact match to your unique shape.

When women tell me what they hate most about gaining weight, the aspect responsible for the most misery is that their clothes don't fit. There is nothing worse than clothes that are too tight. Gouging your waist, binding your belly, digging into your thighs, they are constant, painful reminders of what a failure you are.

Tight clothes continually communicate a negative message. They tell you that you are fat, with "fat" being equivalent to "bad." They do not remind you to watch what you eat so they will be looser. They are punishment. Whenever my weight fluctuates to a point where my clothes feel the least bit tight, I have found that the most positive thing I can do for myself is to buy something that fits my current shape. Frantically trying to lose the excess and forcing myself to be uncomfortable in the meantime does not work nearly as well as being realistic about the present situation. Once my confidence in my attractiveness is restored, my worry about my weight vanishes, and so do the pounds. The truth is, well-fitting size 12's look much better than snug size 10's anyway. Buying clothes that fit you, whatever your current size, is one absolute, concrete step you must take to Clothe Your Spirit. You may not be able to weigh exactly what you want to at this moment, but you can certainly wear clothes that look good on you and that flatter your body.

The first barrier to break through is the belief that the fat on your body is somehow more unpleasant or disfiguring than anyone else's. The reality is, when women gain weight, they rarely do it evenly. The majority of excess weight tends to settle in one area. When weight is distributed unevenly, it makes it more difficult to find clothes that fit. When I gain weight, my waist and midriff thicken but my thighs stay the same, so when I am trying on slacks, if the waist fits, the legs always end up baggy. You may have the opposite problem of full hips and legs and a small torso. No matter how much you gain or lose, your height, the length of your limbs, and the width of your shoulders stay the same, while other areas get larger. If you think this problem is unique to your body, I can assure you that it is practically universal. I know how frustrating it is to try to find clothes. Bigger clothes are not cut to camouflage excesses, they are made for bigger people. But take heart—clothes can be found that are suited to your spirit and will fit you *now*.

The other universal truth about weight gain is that your assets do not disappear when you put on pounds. Even when I am at my heaviest, my hands are still long and tapering, my shoulders delicate, my neck long and well formed, my legs slim, my feet and toes attractive, and my bust generous and sexy. When you gain weight your beauty does not vanish, but you may have to concentrate on actively enhancing it.

Learning to recognize your assets, at whatever your current weight, will help you create an appro-

Getting clothes that fit me made me look so much better that I saw I didn't have to be thinner to have clothes look nice on me. And being thin doesn't guarantee looking good in clothes.
Holly

priate balance in your overall appearance. Putting too much emphasis on a part of your body you are not comfortable with can be a real disadvantage when you are selecting styles of clothing. When you try too hard to camouflage the offending area, the opposite happens: you draw attention to it. For example, a client with a slightly square shape preferred skirts that were a bit loose around the waistband. She felt she should not draw attention to her middle. This made her look as though she had no waist and consequently no shape. When she tried on a dress with a wide, well-fitting belt, her curves were given some definition. Someone with the opposite figure (a tiny waist and full hips) who chooses a wide, gathered skirt to detract from her "problem" area, is actually drawing attention to it by creating an unbalanced proportion.

It *is* difficult to see yourself realistically. The parts of your body you feel ill at ease with become magnified by the extra attention. If you looked at your body without knowing it belonged to you, I am sure you would find yourself far less objectionable. Consciously seeking out your assets will encourage a more accurate balance. The ultimate goal is to see your body as a whole rather than a jumble of parts. Bodies have an amazing symmetry. It might be hard for you to see at first, but you can learn to detach from your displeasure and high expectations, to step back and look at the outline, and to find harmony and balance.

Developing a realistic body image is a problem for nearly all persons regardless of their weight. The next time it seems as if an endless stream of slender women is parading past you, imagine yourself walking up to them and asking them what their secret is. A few will say they watch their diet and exercise regularly. The rest will look at you, startled, and tell you they don't have a secret, because they aren't slim at all. In fact, they have just gained five pounds and their clothes don't fit. As they point to an invisible rear end or a tiny tummy and tell you how self-conscious they feel about it, they won't just be modestly

Before, I never felt quite thin enough, but now I accept where my body is right now because what I have to put on it feels good.

Gloria

preening. Their conviction that they need to lose weight is every bit as sincere as yours.

Feeling fat is much more of an epidemic in our society than being fat. The media has sounded the alarm about overweight as a problem, and newspapers, magazines, and television features have rushed in with diet and exercise-related solutions. But nothing ever addresses the vast mental and physical resources that are lost in the endless crusade for slenderness. In addition to the fact that you will actually look better if you take the emphasis off losing weight, consider how beneficial it will be to your peace of mind. Worrying about your weight takes tremendous concentration and precious energy that vanishes into the weight-loss chasm and is gone forever.

If you want to hang on to believing that improving your body will make you happy until you have reason to believe otherwise, that's fine. It only becomes a barrier if you allow it to keep you from getting started with the process of Clothing Your Spirit. You may want to wait until you are able to exercise more or can afford liposuction before you make a serious commitment to having the wardrobe you want, or you may prefer to put off facing salespeople and other chic shoppers until you feel more confident. But beware! There is just one problem with holding out for a better day.

You might end up waiting forever.

There is no more successful way to get what you desire than to smash through the barrier of wanting and waiting to be thinner. You will notice a change of perspective immediately. When you look at Holly's photographs, the discomfort in the "before" picture is obvious. I did not tell her to look at the camera self-consciously or to round and slouch her shoulders. In the first set of "after" shots, Holly's new-found confidence is apparent. Holly did not begin to lose weight until after she bought clothing that expressed her spirit. "It really helped that I looked good in my new clothes," she said. "My whole self-image started changing. I didn't decide

I can remember when I weighed 118 and I thought I was fat, and when I weighed 122 I thought I was fat, and I can remember weighing 145 and thinking I was fat. It doesn't make any difference. I can look back to when I was really thin or I can just be today. What if I look back in ten years and say, "Oh, I missed the best time in my whole life?" How sad! I may never be any prettier, I may never be any thinner and what if I miss all that by wishing I was different.

Debbie

to lose weight, it just started happening. The clothes suited me then, and they still suit me now. I liked everything so much that when they got too big I had them adjusted so I could still wear them. I could wear a straight skirt now if I wanted to, but full skirts are still me. That's the way I am."

If you are afraid to buy clothes now because they might be too big later, don't allow that barrier to stand in your way any longer. Your spirit is longing to be revealed right now, on this very day. All it needs is your permission. It takes courage to say, "Maybe I don't meet society's idea of perfection, but I still want to wear clothes that are beautiful and express who I am."

2

Money: How to Afford What You Love

If I asked what you would do with a sudden windfall of cash, one of your first, passionate responses would probably be, "Buy clothes!"

Most of us see money, preferably a great deal of money, as the solution to the problem of having nothing to wear. "If only all the clothes I liked weren't so expensive," you sigh. "If only I had a higher-paying job, or a winning lottery ticket. *Then* I would be able to have the wardrobe I want."

There is no question that having plenty of money makes purchasing what you need much easier, but vast riches are not the magic key unlocking the door to looking wonderful, any more than slenderness is. Like waiting to be slender, not having enough money is a good scapegoat for your dissatisfaction and an excellent excuse to keep you from getting started.

The difference between what you have and what you want is not separated by a vast quantity of cash. With careful thought, planning, and consideration, you *can* afford the clothes you love.

What you *cannot* afford is to buy any more clothes that you hang in your closet and never wear.

You *cannot* afford to buy any more clothes that don't fit the needs of your lifestyle.

You *cannot* afford to buy clothes that you don't really love or feel satisfied with, so that you continuously feel the need to buy more.

The real financial excess is in all the clothes in your closet that don't work for you. Expensive mistakes deflate not your bank balance but also your confidence.

No matter how limited your money for clothes, you can create a wardrobe you can be happy with. If you doubt this truth, then you have some personal barriers that need to be looked at. In this chapter, I will examine some of the common financial conflicts and offer solutions that will help you overcome them.

There are three basic spending patterns that entrap women and keep them from achieving their goal of looking wonderful. The first is being unable to justify spending money on their appearance. The second is exactly the reverse—believing that buying "more" is the solution to looking better. The third pattern is being unwilling to be realistic about the kinds of clothing they need and the money they have available to spend on them.

There is a great deal of fear and self-doubt at the root of these conflicts. Recently, I worked with a woman who was part of the small percentage of the population who have the characteristics of a high-fashion model. When I met Cheryl, she was hosting a party dressed very plainly in jeans and a flannel shirt. Despite her astonishing beauty and 5'10" reed-thin body, her look was boring and unattractive. As we talked it became obvious that she loved clothes, but later, when we were going through her closet, there was clearly very little there that she enjoyed wearing. When I questioned her about it she replied, "I have always been concerned about money. I was afraid if I indulged my passion, it would be impossible to stop."

Many women are perpetually on a diet for the same reason. They fear that if they allowed them-

I never thought my clothes were a priority, not for me. They were for the kids, for everyone else, but not for me. For myself, I just got what would get me by.

Gloria

selves what they crave, the floodgates would break loose and there would be no stopping them. Cheryl was afraid that if she opened up to her deepest longings, she would get herself into financial trouble. She needed assurance that her desires were reasonable, and she needed to build confidence within herself that she could be trusted to take care of her needs without going overboard.

Debbie, on the other hand, acted in the opposite way. Her pattern was to continue to "buy" in hopes that she might hit on something she liked. "Whenever I would get dressed," Debbie told me, "I would try on ten things and get depressed because none of them worked. Then I thought I had to buy more because there was nothing in my closet to wear. I would go shopping and buy everything that fit. But I never got it right, so I would keep buying more."

Debbie's spending eventually caused problems. "I was constantly sneaking clothes into the house. I did it because I knew my husband wouldn't approve of the clothes I bought and he would think I was spending too much money, which I was, but I couldn't help myself. And I felt terrible about it. It was no fun having to lie and sneak around. I was sneaking clothes in for five years, right up until I met you."

It was not a desire to turn over a new leaf and become a better person that stopped Debbie from compulsive buying and deceiving her husband. "Now that I know what my look is, I can go shopping with a plan and come home with exactly what I need. I don't decide to buy something just because I am in a store. I go with a real purpose in mind. Before, I would look at the racks and think, 'That looks cute and that looks cute; I think I will try it all on.' Knowing what I am looking for narrows it down. I realized if I was clear about what I wanted, I could go into a store and come away with one or two things and be satisfied. When I know what I need the clothes to do for me, I don't have to come home with ten things."

Whether you feel totally deprived for lack of clothes or guilty about clothes in your closet with the price tags still attached, the prescription is the same. You need to fulfill your needs more exactly. You can learn to trust yourself and satisfy your desires in a positive and appropriate way. When you buy something that looks absolutely wonderful on you and fits in perfectly with your lifestyle, you will not continue to feel the need for more. Upcoming chapters, including "Illuminating Your Spirit," "Lifestyle: Making Your Clothes Work For You," and "Clarifying Your Image" will show you how to do exactly that.

If money is tight for you right now, you have certain decisions to make. Would you be happier with a wide variety of mix and match combinations to choose from, or would you rather wear a few special outfits more frequently? Personally, I prefer to own fewer clothes that I totally love, even if it means wearing them several times a week. I don't go into an office every day, so this choice suits my lifestyle as well as my disposition. If you are on a limited clothing budget you may not be able to have the complete wardrobe of your dreams, but you can still look great every day.

There are always choices to be made, and it is up to you to discover what will make you to feel happy and satisfied. If you always feel vaguely deprived, you are letting other emotions cloud the issue. You must take a realistic look at the needs you have for clothing, consider the money you have available, and shop accordingly.

There are clothes in every price range to fit every budget. I have a young friend living on her own for the first time, and I know it is a struggle for her to make ends meet every month. Her approach to her clothing needs was to ignore them in hopes that they would go away. It became a problem when she would desperately need something new and have no choice other than to go somewhere convenient and buy the item as quickly as possible. I encouraged her to start to plan for her clothing requirements, and to seek out sources where her money would go the farthest. She called the other day and told me triumphantly, "I spent my entire day off at a local discount department store. I tried on piles of clothes, and only bought things I really loved. For $85 I was able to buy two pairs of pants, three shirts, and a sweater. I would have paid that much for a blouse alone at one of the boutiques near my office."

A discount store is not the best solution for everyone. Buying one exquisite blouse at a boutique might be the better choice for you. The most important thing is to be clear about what will satisfy you. Denying your needs is not taking responsibility for yourself. If you deprive yourself for too long, eventually you will not be able to stand it any longer and the dam of denial will burst. The danger here is that your purchase will not satisfy your craving for something great. You are much more likely to find something you love if you truly believe you deserve to own wonderful things.

There have been periods in my life when I wondered how I would manage to dress as well as I felt I should. The most difficult time of all was when I first started out as a wardrobe consultant. During the years prior to my career change into fashion, I worked in public relations, and for five years was co-owner of a small firm. "Take Me Shopping!" (as my wardrobing service was originally called) was started on the side as a part-time venture. I never intended it to be a full-time endeavor, but it ended up that way almost by default. The time came for my partner and me to go our separate ways, and I knew public relations was not a career I wanted to continue to pursue. It was an exhilarating yet frightening transition for me, both emotionally and financially. But I loved helping people feel good about how they looked, so I decided to give "Take Me Shopping!" a real shot. The problem was looking the part.

In order to assure people I knew what I was talking about, I had to dress with flair. I had to be a walking advertisement for myself. Even though my budget was minuscule, I could not settle for bargains that were practical but looked only decent. I shopped very carefully, settled on a few really special things, filled in with whatever rock-bottom bargains I could find, and wore the same things over and over.

My fashion business was my permission to look my best and to buy things I loved. The result of that rocky start-up year: more confidence in myself. When I was with a group I didn't hang back. When I spoke at seminars and all eyes were upon me, I knew I was presenting myself in the best possible way.

You do not need an excuse as specific as mine to justify spending money on clothes. Clothing Your Spirit will benefit every single aspect of your life, from enhancing your relationships with others to increasing your prosperity in business. If you are starting a new job or moving to a new city, Clothing Your Spirit will ease your way by helping you attract like-minded people. If you are going through a difficult transition in your life, Clothing Your Spirit will help you establish and affirm who you are.

The greatest benefit of Clothing Your Spirit is the chance to increase your self-expression. It will dramatically enhance your enjoyment of life. Don't bury this opportunity at the bottom of the bills.

Clothe Your Spirit is much more than just shopping and buying clothes. If you share expenses with a spouse or partner, it may be necessary to explain why you need new clothes before the old ones have worn out. Your challenge is to be straightforward and upfront about this.

Debbie is now honest about her clothing needs and expenditures. "My spending is so much more reasonable now that I can be open with my husband about it. Last fall, I decided I needed a few additional things for work. I told my husband I was going shopping for clothes and he said that was fine. I came home with exactly what I set out to buy: a suit, a blouse, a skirt, and a dress. And that was it. He didn't blink an eye. He just said, 'I hope that's enough,' and it has been. I don't have to sneak or apologize or pretend like I didn't buy it. I just walked in the door and said, 'Here it is!'

Concentrating on clothing my spirit has made me more prosperous, because I brought my image up to where it needed to be. I feel like I can demand more for my services and get it.
Holly

If I let myself get into a way of thinking in which I go too long without buying clothes, I lose my confidence as far as clothing goes.
Gloria

"The other day I told him I was having a clothes attack, and that I was probably going to have to go and satisfy it sometime in the not-too-distant future. He just said, 'You know how much money there is, so when you are ready, go and do it.' He still doesn't see why I have to add to my summer wardrobe when he only buys a suit every few years, but he is more understanding about it. I understand his financial priorities and he understands clothes are a need for me, so it is a compromise, a meeting that we never would have had before.

"It feels great not to have to sneak. I don't feel like I am cheating, that I have to lie about things. It makes me feel so much better about myself. What a difference, it's wonderful! I feel like a new person."

Give the people close to you an opportunity to learn what Clothing Your Spirit means to you. Encourage them to experience the process for themselves. Men often react in a stereotypical way because they feel it is expected of them, but when given the opportunity, they can find tremendous gratification in the liberating experience Clothe Your Spirit can provide.

Don't be afraid that others will think less of you for giving your appearance a higher priority. Your need for self-expression and your desire to look beautiful is nothing to be ashamed of. It is not a vain, selfish, or silly luxury. Experiencing your beauty is one of the joys of being alive. Spending money on clothes isn't wasteful, especially when you learn to achieve the most satisfaction for your dollar. If you give as much consideration to your wardrobe budget as you do with any financial investment, it will pay off handsomely.

3

Family Roles and Relationships

I can't believe I had such beautiful daughter.
My Mother

Where did she get those big boobs? **My Aunt**

You are fat and ugly. **My Brother**

Everything you have ever heard about your looks during your lifetime contributes to the picture you form in your mind called your self-image. We internalize most of what we hear when we are younger without ever questioning its validity. The comments we receive as adults from friends, lovers, and strangers are scrutinized for accuracy, but nevertheless take their place in our developing self-concept. Good or bad, right or wrong, most of what you think about yourself today has origins in the past. When you Clothe Your Spirit you will want to connect with the essence of the real you. Part of this process involves untangling yourself from the intricate web of your former roles and beliefs.

When I was growing up, my parents told me I was pretty, and it never occurred to me to question whether I was or wasn't. With the exception of adolescent acne and braces, I have never been critical of my face, and I have always considered myself to be basically attractive. My feelings about my body were another story. When my younger brother taunted me by saying I was fat and ugly, I dismissed the "ugly" and concerned myself with the "fat." In my family, "fat" was the one thing you should not become. The adults in my life were always fearful of being overweight, and I vividly recall my mother and her friends discussing how none of them could eat over eight hundred calories without gaining weight. I did not want to be fat either, so I anxiously adopted their belief system. I wasn't fat, but I was afraid I would be.

My fifteen-year-old body was already an object for discussion. I was the first woman in my family to have large breasts, and they were often commented upon. I was different. I was encouraged to dress in a way so as not to draw too much attention to them. Then I did get fat, and my breasts were no longer an issue.

It was not until many years later that I stopped to consider for myself how I really felt about my own body. Were my breasts really so conspicuous? They are generous, certainly, but they do not compare to the "assets" of Dolly Parton. I realized it was up to me to decide if I wanted to emphasize them or not. Now I think of them in a positive way; they are pretty and they give my clothes a lovely shape. What's more, they are a part of me that reflects my sensuous and womanly spirit. When I stopped trying to hide them under baggy sweaters, I was surprised to discover that just below them was a slender and attractive midriff. Learning that I wasn't completely "top heavy" changed my concept of the type of clothing I could wear. When I developed a more realistic body image I could choose styles that flattered my curves rather than disguised them.

Now is your chance to objectively examine some

of the things you have been told. As you read this chapter your mind will be flooded with memories of past compliments, stings, and insults. As they surface, you might find it useful to jot them down for later scrutiny. Something that might have been true about you in the past may no longer be correct. You don't have to believe anything about yourself that is not absolutely accurate. As Eleanor Roosevelt once said, "No one can make you feel inferior without your consent."

In addition to all the remarks that you responded to and internalized, you probably had a role within your family, such as the "smart one," the "rebellious one," or the "pretty one." Whenever I work with a woman who is attractive but obviously not making the most of her assets, I try to discover what past influences might be the cause. Katharine told me a story that many women with sisters can probably relate to.

"I am the oldest child in my family, and my younger sister grew up in my shadow. I was given a lot of encouragement and from an early age I displayed considerable talent. I danced beautifully, and I always did exceptionally well in school. I was a pretty little girl, but as I grew older the emphasis shifted away from my appearance. My younger sister, on the other hand, was not nearly as accomplished, so she received more attention for her looks. It felt balanced and fair for her to be the 'pretty one' and for me to be the 'smart one.' After a while I never concerned myself with how I looked. Once established, this pattern followed me into my adult life. I went into business with a woman partner who was both beautiful and intelligent, but once again I was the more accomplished of the two of us. It felt natural for her to capture the attention for her beauty. I dressed very conservatively to emphasize that I was to be taken seriously."

Many of us have grown up believing that somehow it is not possible to be both intelligent, warm, caring, compassionate *and* beautiful. After Katharine and I worked together to clothe her spirit,

My father always teased me about being small. He wanted a voluptuous daughter. That made me feel inadequate. I always thought, "Why did I have to get cheated?" But when I had my son I had big breasts, and I hated them, so I decided I liked having little breasts. That's what changed it all.

Debbie

allowing her feminine and romantic nature to emerge, she discovered the joy of pairing her many intellectual gifts with her soft and gentle beauty. Expressing the loveliness of her spirit has in no way detracted from her ability to be taken seriously.

"My clients are quite taken with my new clothes. They comment on how feminine I look, and I can see they are looking at me in a whole new way. Yesterday I caught a glimpse of myself in the mirror, and I thought, 'What a remarkable face.' I feel as if I have discovered a completely new aspect of myself. Now that I know I am a lovely and romantic-looking woman, it has given me permission to be, and say, and do all kinds of things. It has allowed me to be more vulnerable and gentle than I ever was before, to take more risks, and to be more feminine about solving problems."

Katharine discovered she did not have to limit herself to being the "smart one." The patterns set in childhood can have a strong and long-lasting hold on us. It is never too late to re-examine their validity and push through old barriers.

Believing that you cannot be both smart and beautiful may have been only one of the attitudes you grew up with. I was told that putting too much emphasis on my looks was shallow. When I was in high school, my girlfriends and I spent hours on our clothes, hair, and make-up. I am sure I was excrutiatingly boring to everyone but my peers. My mother made it clear how vain and superficial she thought I was. Her opinion really mattered to me, and I was stung. For many years I felt vaguely guilty, thinking that I was overly concerned with my appearance. When I switched careers to become an image consultant, I worried that my mother would look down on my work, but she was the first in line to "have her colors done." It is now clear to me that she is proud of both my beauty and my accomplishments. The pressure and judgments I feared were part of my past.

My interest in clothing was not initially encouraged, but in many other families just the opposite is true. I have heard stories of mothers pressuring their daughters to dress in a certain way, or to pay attention to fashion and style when they were obviously disinterested.

When I met Holly she admitted her plain way of dressing started as rebellion against her mother.

"When I was a kid I didn't care about what I wore," Holly told me. "When I was a teenager, mini-skirts were coming in and my mother always wanted me to be 'in' with the crowd. I never wanted to be; I never wanted to be 'mod.' My mother would hem up my dresses and I would never wear them. I still don't like to be pushed into anything, but I will choose something stylish now if I feel it's really 'me.' "

When Holly took some of her new clothes home during her last visit, her mother was quite impressed. " 'Why wouldn't you do that as a child?' my mother asked me. I guess I just wanted to do it my own way.

"My brothers were really shocked when they saw the pictures you took of me. 'That's not my little sister; it can't be!' they said. Both my brothers were jocks, and I was always their plain-Jane sister. When I was younger and they drove me somewhere, they would make me hide under the front seat so none of their friends could see me with them. It makes me feel great to show them they were wrong."

Our growing-up years are not the only time when we are influenced by our family structure. A woman may feel confident about her self-image until she marries. If she is overly anxious to please her husband and win his approval, over the years her sense of self may become blurred or buried. Gloria told me the effect her twenty-five-year marriage had had on her confidence. Even though the marriage was over, her husband's influence still remained.

"Before I was married I felt very comfortable in my big full skirts with crinolines and cashmere sweaters. I loved pinks and blues. After I was married it was important to me that I look right for my husband, and I always wanted to look perfect for

My mother would dress me the way she wanted to look, which was totally opposite of how I wanted to look. When I was five, I used to try to hide my clothes from my mother because I didn't like the colors. She would pick really loud prints; I remember this one dress, it had red and white valentine hearts on it and I hated it.
Serita

every social occasion. He would go shopping with me and help me pick out what to wear for an occasion because I had no confidence. But his image of me was different from mine, and sometimes I wore what he wanted me to wear and not what I thought made me look better. He thought I was a taller, bigger person. He liked me in gold and beige. I still remember a beige 'After-Five' suit he picked out for me. Whenever I bought something for myself, even if I liked it, I never felt secure. After I was on my own again, I started to pick out what I wanted, but my confidence and self-esteem were so low. As you can see, the results were pretty dismal."

Interestingly enough, the only time Gloria felt comfortable was when she was pregnant. "I had really nice maternity clothes, and I always chose my own. My husband wasn't so concerned with what I wore so I felt I could be more myself. I enjoyed my pregnancies."

During child-rearing years, it can be easy to let the role of "mom" take over. New school clothes come first, and life takes on a different focus. But eventually the kids grow up. A large percentage of my clients are women in their late 40's and 50's who have finished raising their families, and who are ready to turn the spotlight on themselves. What a wonderful time to Clothe Your Spirit! It is an opportunity to reaffirm yourself and enhance the next phase of life. The kids are usually tremendously impressed to see their parent in a new way.

Whenever clients and I go shopping, they always have twinges of concern about how their new purchases will be received. "What will my mother, my co-workers, my boyfriend, my kids think?" The changes are almost universally greeted with applause and praise. "Why didn't you do this earlier?" responded Gloria's boyfriend. On their way home from a party, Debbie's husband told her she was the best-dressed person there. "That is the first time he has ever said that," she said. "He told me I was the prettiest person at the whole party. It was wonderful." The most common response from a loved one to my clients is, ''That is exactly what I had in mind, how I always felt you should look. I just didn't know how to help you do it.''

We want people to like us, to find us attractive and pleasing. When we express our true nature, we give them the best opportunity that we can. As you focus more and more on dressing for self-expression, the important people in your life will respond to the unequivocal ''rightness'' of your new look. They love to see a physical manifestation of the inner person they know so well.

I could fill this book with stories about family roles and relationships. Every person I have ever worked with has had a story to tell. We all do. No matter what you were brought up hearing, thinking, or believing, now you can ~~now~~ be whomever you want to be. You don't have to go along with anyone's idea of the correct role for you, whether it is your parent's, sibling's, husband's, or children's. When you Clothe Your Spirit, there is no need to rebel or conform. You can sift through the past and search for what is really you.

PART TWO

Discovering Your Uniqueness

Illuminating Your Spirit

Now is the time to discover the individual nature of your spirit and become "known" to yourself. Projecting the essence of what is uniquely you through the way you dress is the heart of the Clothe Your Spirit process. Your spirit can be described in a way that is easily translated into fashion terms. Understanding how your spirit relates to fashion is extremely helpful in clarifying your wardrobe selection process. When faced with thousands of options every time you walk into a store, having a sense of what is appropriate for you streamlines the process of choosing. Seeing the latest fashion trends will no longer cause you to apprehensively wonder, "Am I right for the new looks?" Instead you will have the freedom to ask, "Is the look right for *me*?"

Deep down, you know how special you really are. Your challenge is to bring that specialness to the surface. To describe your spirit, begin by considering your physical attributes, your personality, and your character traits. Each person's combination of characteristics is as unique as his or her fingerprints. Looking at how all the aspects of your physical and

"It is the feeling of being known for who you are that makes Clothe Your Spirit so wonderful."
Debbie

emotional being fit together will lead to the discovery of your "fashion spirit." This discovery will not be assigned to you, and you will not be asked to find yourself within pre-determined categories. You will decide for yourself what combination of terms best suits your spirit.

Describing your spirit is not a mysterious or metaphysical endeavor—it simply requires an adjustment in perspective. Deep and profound insights are not required. Your understanding will evolve as you work with this new idea, but your own intuition will help to get you started. Imagine yourself as a giant jigsaw puzzle. Spill the pieces onto the floor and look down at the jumble of shapes and sizes. As you examine each piece and attempt to fit it to a corresponding shape, you will see aspects of yourself as if for the first time. The exercises at the conclusion of this chapter will help you assemble the pieces to form a unified picture.

It is a rare and wonderful feeling to define for *yourself* what is really *you*. Unlike a restrictive label, the terms you choose will feel exactly right to you. "I feel as if I've come home" is the way my clients often describe the experience of getting in touch with their spirits. When their clothes communicate correctly, clients emerge from the dressing room, stare in the mirror at their new ensembles, and declare, "It's *me*!"

The terms you choose to describe your spirit should have specific meaning when applied to a clothing style. As you seek a definition of your spirit, it is important to remember that not every quality you possess will relate directly to fashion. The terms must be a synthesis of both inner and outer qualities. Being loving, intelligent, or caring are wonderful characteristics, but when considered independently they will not be much help to you as you are making clothing decisions.

Let me use what I have discovered about myself as an illustration. In attempting to describe my spirit, I chose a few clear and simple terms that sum up how I feel about who I am. I also take into consideration my physical appearance. I have interpreted the following terms in a way that has meaning for me when I apply them to a fashion style.

The key words I feel best describe my spirit (coincidentally) all start with the letter "S": *straightforward, sensuous, sophisticated,* and *sparkling.* There are many other descriptive terms that I can readily identify with, but the above four adjectives are a distillation. These words have personal meanings to me, as the definition of your spirit will to you. I have other qualities I often want to express, such as sportiness, friendliness, refinement, elegance, glamour, and drama, but I don't connect emotionally with them in the same way. They are moods rather than expressions of who I am. When I hit upon the above words, in my heart I knew they were right for me. When I look in the mirror I see a face that is both sophisticated and sparkling, and a body and demeanor that is at the same time straightforward and sensuous.

I have my own personal understanding for each of the following terms:

Sensuous: I am sensuous looking, but I am also very attuned to my senses (the definition of sensuous). The look, the feel, the taste of things constantly absorb me and enrich my existence. There is no getting around the fact that I have attributes that are considered "sexy": "bedroom eyes," full lips (which as a teenager I loathed), and quite a curvy, voluptuous upper body. During a style analysis I was once told that I looked romantic. I assumed this was a demure way of saying sexy. Romantic never felt right. It connotes an ethereal, gentle, gauzy, delicate quality that I do not possess. Sensuous describes a fashion style that more accurately suits me.

Straightforward: Even though I have large breasts, my body is not curvy everywhere. My waist and hips are quite straight. I consider this to be a physically straightforward quality, corresponding to my straightforward manner. I honestly believe that if I had been endowed with an hourglass figure, I would have grown up to be a different person. I would have chosen fluid, flowing skirts and dresses to play up my assets. Dressed in such a way I would have felt more feminine, more charming. Instead, I wear pants or slacks much of the time, which feels more straightforward. Can you imagine anyone more straightforward or no-nonsense than Katherine Hepburn? Her outfit of choice has always been slacks. Once during a workshop I asked the group to describe what they thought was my spirit. One of the participants said "stunning." I was flattered thinking she meant my looks, until she clarified, saying that it was the way in which I said things—that they often stunned people. She was actually making a comment on my straightforward manner.

Sophisticated: I can not recall a time when I did not feel more sophisticated than my peers. Having always looked older than my chronological years, it was a relief to reach my late twenties and have my experience start to catch up with my looks. Growing up in the casual atmosphere of Southern California, I may not have had much of a feel for chic sophistication, but I certainly never looked like the sunny, breezy, much admired "California Girl." As I grew older, I stopped being disappointed about not having waist-length, straight blond hair, and I realized that I had other things going for me. I have long, delicate bones, and some features that are classically elegant. My refined qualities help sophisticated styles look appropriate. My coloring is strong and vivid, allowing me to carry off a measure of drama.

Sparkling: I am only sophisticated up to a point—it is not long before my animated personality announces itelf. No matter how cool I try to be, my sparkle always takes over. I talk fast, I gesture with my hands when I am excited, and I turn red when I am embarrassed. I do not have chiseled features and a calm regal grace, and no amount of ironing in the 1960's tamed my curly hair.

Let me show you how I translate straightforward,

sophisticated, sensuous, and sparkling into fashion terms. I already mentioned that 'straightforward' means to me: no-nonsense types of clothing, especially slacks. Other types of clothing can look straightforward as well. They are simple in design, without a lot of detailing, artifice, or complicated lines. The fabric is either a subtly woven pattern or a solid color. Straightforward fashions are devoid of trendiness. On the right person they can be stunning, on the wrong person absolutely boring.

Sensuous clothing is usually constructed of soft fabric that moves with the body. It drapes and flows over the feminine figure, and is designed so that womanly curves give the garment shape. Sensuous clothing can be classic or romantic, dressy or casual, simple or elaborate. People are often drawn to sensuous clothing because it feels wonderful against the skin. The designs of Donna Karan are some of the most sensuous clothing available. Her first independent collection introduced us to cashmere body suits, worn with simple wrap skirts. Every piece emphasized the body, and not necessarily the very thin body. When her designs began appearing several years ago, excitement pulsed through me. I did not feel the need to rush out to buy them, but it was thrilling to see a new fashion that I felt so connected with.

My response to Karan's fashions gave me new insight and awareness into my spirit. What I saw in her fashions was a sensuous rather than a romantic quality, an emphasis on simplicity instead of on detailing. Previously the emphasis on the feminine leaned more toward the romantic. Dropped waists, delicate shirring, gauzy fabrics, ruffles, and lace have all made a comeback, popularized by designers such as Jessica McClintock. Although my looks might be described as romantic, I would never feel comfortable in that style of clothing.

Sophistication in clothing implies being chic, worldly, up on trends, and clever at putting things together. In that sense, we all want to look sophisticated, especially if it implies knowledge or talent.

The terms "classic" and "romantic" seem exactly right to me. I am also very feminine. I love frilly, lacy, victorian kinds of things.

Serita

My own personal understanding of sophistication coaxes the meaning of straightforward a step further, implying the elegance of simple beauty, combined with the forward-looking quality of new and inventive designs.

It would be easy for me to err on the side of looking too sophisticated. Anything overly sophisticated or severe "wears" me. I am not cool, composed, or regal enough to carry such designs off. The sparkling side of my spirit, including my curly hair and animated expression, belie any kind of overly sophisticated look I might attempt. My sparkling spirit is a bright, fresh aliveness that helps balance the sensuous, straightforward, and sophisticated expression of my spirit.

I can tell when something is overly sophisticated for me, or too sexy/sensuous, or even too bright and playful. I love the fun, delightful clothes some of my clients wear, but on me they look silly and I feel dumpy.

Recently, I was explaining the idea of defining your spirit to a new client, and telling her about the terms I had chosen for myself. She replied, "Doesn't everyone want to be sophisticated and sensuous? Isn't that an ideal?" The answer is no. Attractiveness is unique to every individual. A person's charm can be in her freshness, vitality, delicacy, richness, or intensity.

My spirit is fun, personable—a "little kid" type. I feel both feminine and girlish. I'm not ruffly, but I will wear something with lots of colors or unique little patterns that is girlish. I am also very responsible. The clothes I wear to work, even though they are fun, are still professional.

Holly

As a comparison to my self-evaluation, I want to introduce you to Susan, a delightful young woman in her early thirties. When she arrived for her first appointment dressed in overalls and a t-shirt, I mistakenly assumed that she was about twenty-two. I was drawn to her breezy friendliness right away, but any sign of Susan's femininity or maturity were well-hidden beneath her boyish attire. I wanted to help Susan retain her fresh and appealing naturalness, but also to help her express other aspects of herself more fully. She was anxious to dress in a more appropriate way, but felt trapped inside the image she had created for herself.

I am going to let Susan tell you, in her own words,

what she discovered about herself, her spirit, and her relationship to clothing. (All the words that play a part in the final definition of her spirit are highlighted.)

"I see myself as a spring flower. I love spring—green grass, Easter eggs, and bunnies. My favorite color is robin's egg blue. Of all the spring flowers, I relate most to the golden poppy. It is *strong* and *exuberant*, like me. I wouldn't necessarily wear that golden color, but I love what the flower represents for me.

"My skin reminds me of a peach, because peaches have a blush on them, and they are fun to touch. My eyes are like jade, with grey in them. Kind of like the ocean. They reflect the other side of me, the side that is *introspective*, intelligent, aesthetic, foggy. Sometimes I tell myself, 'I am the spy with the jade-green eyes.' I have always wanted to be *mysterious*, inscrutable. I have fantasies about slinking around, being 'in the know.'

"I can really connect to these different parts of myself, especially when I see how they all fit together. My hair, which I used to hate, reminds me of seaweed and mermaids—more ocean images. My hair is translucent, like being under water.

"Thinking about making the most of my assets, instead of just hiding my flaws, has made a big difference for me. I have become aware that my upper body is very much an asset. It is not custie-doll tiny, but it is very *feminine*. I am medium-boned and *graceful*. I have been told by people that I am soft, but that never meant anything to me. I see now that my body is not angular, nor is it round. It is *soft*.

"To be soft and feminine is really a new thing for me. I always associated soft with weak. I couldn't stand the idea of being a weak female, so I rejected my feminine side entirely. I felt like a boy. I dressed like a boy. I used to buy most of my clothes in the men's department.

"Now I have disengaged soft from weak. I still feel the best in clothes that are sporty, but they are no longer rugged or crude.

"When we were working with the colors, styles, and fabrics that would look best on me, I felt myself really responding to key words. Words that described colors like *clear* and *fresh* or textural words like *crisp* and *clean* set up a whole chain of images for me. Those words made sense to me in terms of clothing, but they also really click into my spirit. My connection with them gives me permission to assert my own spirit into my clothing choices.

"When I am shopping now I always remind myself of the words '*clear*' (my coloring) and '*medium*' (my build). I really have terms and images locked into place. I have adjectives that fit my brand of liveliness, my individual spirit. My spirit is *fresh*, *crisp*, *vibrant*, *playful*, *fun*, and *perky*, with an *edge of mystery*."

Susan's experience of discovery was uniquely her own. Fresh . . . crisp . . . vibrant . . . playful . . . a bit mysterious—you can feel a sense of what she must be like. The terms sophisticated and sensuous would hold no appeal for her. In fact, if someone criticized Susan and told her she should grow up and dress in a more sophisticated way, she would probably rebel and head back to the boy's department.

Discovering the words for yourself inspires a great sense of loyalty to them. Because you, and only you, are describing the qualities of your being, you have the option to change them if they no longer feel exactly right.

And change they will. Human beings are ever dynamic and evolutionary. As we move through stages of life we have a corresponding need to express our inner growth.

Just as I believe a person's character is formed at an early age, I also believe the basic components of her spirit remain the same. The degree, or balance, shifts and adjusts. As we mature, what we want from clothing evolves with our feelings. It is obvious to us when someone is not "dressing her age." We no longer have rigid rules of appropriateness for certain age groups, but we feel uneasy when someone disregards her years. When I was younger, I knew I looked mature, but I would have felt uncomfortable reflecting an outer sophistication that I had yet to emotionally acquire.

It is often hard to readjust a balance after it has been "set" for any length of time. If for whatever reason you feel the need to adopt a certain self-image, it can soon feel as if that image is you, even if it is not the essence of your spirit. I have met many women for whom the need to be serious or to be taken seriously has throughly overshadowed their otherwise playful, romantic, or feminine natures. When I bring this to their attention through my observations about their spirits, they are often willing to embrace a freer aspect of themselves. When given permission to be expressed, an area that has been repressed often blossoms and bursts forth. In my case, I denied my sophistication for so long that I felt my attractiveness was based on my "sparkling" brand of animation. I thought bold, bright colors and striking styles were my best bet. When I started working with the Clothe Your Spirit concept I became more in touch with other aspects of my self and began to feel comfortable wearing clothes that were softer and more sophisticated. As a result, I felt my energy calm down and my dealings with others grow more confident and relaxed.

My spirit is the glowing part of me, ready to face new things and adventures in life. I would describe it as classic, gentle, glowing, sunny, and funny.

Gloria

Susan describes a similar experience of using aspects of her spirit to balance her life in other ways. "There is a subtlety to my coloring, which I can appreciate now because I am learning to be subtle. I realize that I don't always have to hit people over the head with a sledge hammer. I am using my clothing to help me feel more balanced. I don't have to be either hyper and intense or a crushed flower. I am aiming for something in the middle. It is okay to just cruise and to be in touch with me. I also see this is just a beginning, there is plenty of me to unfold. And it will come—I don't have to go after it."

As your awareness of the connection between your inner and outer characteristics strengthens, you will find yourself more connected to the body you are attempting to clothe. When that happens, two magical transformations will occur. First, you may actually like something about yourself that you previously regarded with distaste—perhaps freckles, full lips, hair color, curvy hips, or strong legs. Second, the magnitude of displeasure you feel towards an area you are less than happy with will shrink to reasonable proportions. When you look in the mirror you will see yourself in a realistic and less distorted way. When you can discover your assets and regard your body accurately, the clothes you select will truly flatter you.

If you use your imagination, it is possible to connect any aspect of your body to an inner characteristic. It has always frustrated me that my tummy has never been, nor ever will be, flat and firm. It is easy enough to camouflage, but I wondered if I could make any kind of positive connection with it. I concluded that my rounded belly expressed the side of me that is nurturing. Elegance and sophistication aside, I am a warm, loving, even motherly, person. I cannot honestly say I now love my midriff bulge and have stopped doing sit-ups forever, but the feeling of dislike and disgust have eased into a kinder acceptance.

When you Clothe Your Spirit, you can use what appeals to you in fashion to tell you more about yourself. If you observe the choices you make, they will give you a path to your subconscious. You are communicating who you are through your clothing, and sometimes what you feel a need to express might surprise you. You have the opportunity to open a door on a new aspect of yourself.

You can carry the psychological aspect of Clothe Your Spirit as far as you wish, or you can choose to downplay it completely. Not everyone feels comfortable with intense personal exploration and self-scrutiny. It is a vehicle you have available to you when you Clothe Your Spirit, but it is just as valid to make several simple connections that will streamline the clothes-selection process for you.

Remember, even if you exhaustively explore your

spirit, searching for many subtle nuances and connections, you are still going to be working with only a few clear and simple terms. It is a question of preference whether you distill a great deal of information or work with what seems immediately obvious to you. The choice is yours.

Not every piece of clothing has to reflect all the aspects of your spirit. It is the overall look and feeling of the complete outfit that you are after. Some outfits will express a balance of qualities, some only one. The terms you choose are to be used as guidelines, not mandates. The concept is designed to be helpful, not limiting. We love variety, and it is a pleasure to play with a look for the sheer fun of it. You can still follow trends, experiment with new ideas. We all get in moods when we want to be someone else. Wearing a costume can be delightful and is always an option. Clothing serves many different purposes: You may want to stop a conversation at a party, disappear into a crowd, appear extremely conservative or businesslike. Your spirit terms are your "home base." There is no need to feel guilty if at times you feel like leaving for a short vacation.

I was never sure about who I was, so I had all these things that worked when I was in the mood, but when I wasn't in the mood they didn't work. Now my clothes are a combination of all those people that I am—impish, sophisticated, dramatic, and sleek.

Debbie

As you begin to work with the Clothe Your Spirit approach, you will find yourself having more fun with clothes. When you know what direction to move in, frustration and confusion will be replaced by a sense of inner satisfaction. It will still aggravate you when you are unable to find what you are looking for, but you will no longer waste precious energy trying to adjust yourself to something that does not suit you.

If you find yourself becoming overwhelmed by the thought of choosing terms that express your spirit, you will defeat the goal of finding ease and pleasure in the clothing-selection process. Take your time. Don't worry about finding an exact definition or doing it wrong. Just thinking about it will provoke glimmers of insight. Remember, the terms you are looking for need only to have personal meaning for you. In order to help strengthen your sense of individuality and uniqueness, now is a good time to compare yourself to others, noticing how you differ. When you look at the women featured in this book, do you find you feel closer to Debbie, Holly, Gloria, or Serita? Or perhaps Loie, Marilyn, Karen, Christy, or Patty?

Take the process of identifying your spirit terms as far as you can. As Susan so wisely said, "I see this as just a beginning; there is plenty of me to unfold. And it will come—I don't have to go after it."

5

How Am I Special?

Before you start to clarify your spirit in relationship to fashion, it is important to understand the approach to take. Looking closely at yourself is not the same as picking yourself apart with scientific accuracy. The light you use to illuminate your understanding should be a rosy soft-glow, not the harsh glare of an ordinary naked florescent. Now is not the time to steel yourself, stand in front of a full-length mirror, and face the music.

The purpose of the following exercise is to put into words some of the feelings you have about your inner and outer characteristics. You will be attaching descriptive terms to qualities you instinctively know you possess. There is a world of difference between words that are technically accurate and words that are emotionally descriptive. To help you understand the kind of words to use, I have formulated lists of adjectives that will stimulate your thinking. The goal of this exploration is to uncover words you connect with, not to try to guess which of my incomplete list of terms you come the closest to.

Let go of how you think you apppear to others,

and tune into your inner responses to the words you see. The terms you choose should touch you. Some will leap off the page, and others will slowly steal into your heart. When you hit upon a word that connects with your spirit, it will resonate, thumping a clear chord of recognition inside you.

For those of you who have never had a kind word to say about yourselves, this will be difficult at first. I have done this exercise with many groups of women, and although I carefully explain the kinds of adjectives to use, I still see lists that contain only "fat" and "overweight" as their responses. If you have lived a lifetime thinking you must be honest and critical about your flaws, it is hard to change your way of thinking. When you begin, you may draw a blank, but stay with it. Discovering your fashion spirit will be worth it.

DISCOVERING YOUR SPIRIT EXERCISE

Through a series of written steps you will be developing an idea of your spirit in relationship to fashion. Read completely through the instructions, and then work through them in the order they appear.

1. Get out a pencil and paper. The actual act of writing things down will stimulate your mind to probe new areas. The brain is unable to move into unchartered territory when it is trying to retain previous information. Writing ideas down allows you to continually clean and freshen your slate.

2. Before you read any farther, jot down any terms that may have leapt into your mind when you were reading my examples. Your initial, uncensored responses are usually very truthful. Are there any words that immediately come to mind that describe you?

3. Take out three fresh pieces of paper. Title page one "Physical Attributes," page two "Inner Quali-

ties," and page three "My Spirit." You are now going to write lists of adjectives about yourself on pages one and two. Put page three aside for now.

4. Concentrate on "Physical Attributes" for a moment. To get started, list any physical characteristic you can think of about yourself. Areas to concentrate on include: the overall look of your body; your walk; your bone structure (look at your shoulders, arms, legs, hands, and feet); the shape of your face and your facial features (eyes, mouth, nose); and your coloring. Do keep in mind the difference between words that are simply accurate and adjectives that are emotionally descriptive. For example, if you are tall, are you lanky, rangy, graceful, powerful, or streamlined? If you are small in stature, are you dainty, sturdy, or compact? If you look in the mirror at your eyes, first you will notice the color, but also notice if they are soft, gentle, intense, or deep. My list of adjectives will get you thinking in the right direction, but feel free to come up with your own.

5. Create a list of your inner characteristics on your second page. What kind of personality do you have? What are your inner strengths? What qualities are you especially proud of? Describe the kind of person you are. Some words will help you discover your spirit in relation to clothing, others will not. For now, don't censor them. Thinking of one quality might alert you to another.

6. Compare your lists. See if any of the terms overlap. This is not necessarily obvious. Use your imagination, stretch a bit. Remember, I considered my straight hips in relation to my straightforward manner. Other examples of words that can relate to each other include: compact-direct, delicate-romantic, curved-gracious, fresh-natural, and strong-determined. A small sampling of words that can describe both inner and outer characteristics include striking, vibrant, soft, gentle, deep, and bright. Put any terms

that you feel capture the essence of who you are on page three, the one titled "My Spirit." Run down the list of terms and add any ones that you especially like. Look over your previous pages and see if you can discover any relationships.

7. Think of your terms in combination with each other. No single term used alone is going to feel just right. The individual combination is what describes your uniqueness. "Romantic" takes on a different meaning when combined with "sensuous gypsy" or "classic innocence." "Calm-sporty-traditional" or "calm-serene-gentle" conjure up different images.

8. Do not do the following step until you have completed steps one through seven. Otherwise you will identify a fashion style you like without connecting to the true essence of your spirit. In order to help you, the terms you choose must come from the heart. When you feel you have gone as far as you can with the above exercises, then look over the page of fashion terms. Identify the fashion styles which are the closest to the list of terms you created to describe your spirit. Some may even match exactly.

9. You can gain additional insight by thinking about the clothing you currently own. Forget about your inner self for a minute, and think specifically about clothes you own or clothing that appeals to you. What is it about your favorite pieces that make them wonderful? Are they soft, easy, free flowing, streamlined, delicate? Jot down these terms as well.

10. If you cannot figure out what you are, figure out what you are not. I know I am definitely not "earthy," nor am I "childlike." My body is not sturdy, and my nose is not pert. Go through the lists and cross out everything that feels absolutely wrong. Make a list of "maybes" from the terms that are left. After you have eliminated some of the list, go back and respond to the remaining terms. See if you feel closer to some of the "maybes" than to others.

11. If you have selected several words, roll them over in your mind and notice your response. They should continue to feel honest and true. If something doesn't feel right, go back for a little fine tuning. Remember to select terms that describe the different key elements of your spirit. Be careful not to choose different adjectives that mean the same thing. You are much too complex and multi-faceted to feel satisfied with a limited definition for long.

If you are not blinded by great flashes of insight, do not be disheartened. Any new exercise takes practice. Now that you know what to look for, observe your dealings with clothing. Even though the instructions are straightforward and make it appear that you can sit right down and do this, you may in fact need to set up the framework and continue to think about it for awhile. Start with a few insights, and add to them.

ADJECTIVES DESCRIBING PHYSICAL ATTRIBUTES

Overall Body Design:
curvy, angular, voluptuous, sumptuous, sensuous, straight, streamlined, lanky, long, sinewy, compact, sturdy, delicate, dainty, petite, soft, ripe, luscious

Shoulders:
broad, straight, rounded, delicate, narrow, strong, squared

Legs:
long, strong, slender, curvy, straight, powerful

Walk:
quick, languorous, bouncy, boyish, athletic, leisurely, brisk, direct, sexy, swinging

Face Shape:
soft, rounded, angular, curved, open, broad, heart-shaped, delicate, slender, long

Mouth/Smile:
sexy, pert, bright, charming, slow, funny, winning, brilliant, sparkling, dazzling, pouty, determined, mobile, animated, spirited, fresh

Nose:
strong, elegant, pert, perky, dramatic, distinctive, classic, aquiline

Eyes:
twinkling, sparkling, intense, soft, gentle, kind, deep, sultry, sharp, bright, mysterious, expressive, wishful, eager, open, humorous, animated, clear, soulful, muted, molten

Hands/Feet:
long, elegant, graceful, delicate, strong, sturdy

Coloring:
dark, strong, delicate, fresh, healthy, intense, gentle, muted, soft, quiet, dramatic, warm, cool, subtle, deep, peachy, rosy, vibrant, striking, glowing, burnished, rich

ADJECTIVES DESCRIBING YOUR SPIRIT

feminine, womanly, gracious, serene, gentle, delicate, classic, romantic, fun, funny, childlike, little-kid, youthful, fresh, friendly, lively, bubbly, pixie, sprite

light, bright, light-hearted, clear, simple, cheerful, open, innocent, wholesome, eager, animated, mischievous, exuberant, charming, daring, wild, adventurous, racy, subtle

natural, relaxed, casual, warm, rich, solid, earthy, true, honest, complex, thoughtful, wise, sincere, gypsy, athletic, movable, moving, energetic, strong

vibrant, free flowing, free spirit, crackling, snappy, sparkling, artistic, creative, dynamic, buoyant, whimsical, traditional, conservative, straight, precise, rooted, grounded, formal, informal

elegant, refined, dramatic, sophisticated, intense, straightforward, streamlined, glittering, queenly, regal, princesslike, sensuous, ripe, luscious, fluid, spirited, playful, impish, zany, frolicsome, vivacious

FASHION TERMS

sophisticated, straightforward, free flowing, earthy, classic, traditional, sturdy, rugged, athletic, simple, fresh, charming, clean, streamlined, delicate, romantic, crisp, casual, relaxed, informal

feminine, sexy, sensuous, graceful, dramatic, daring, striking, formal, wild, crazy, fun, tailored, conservative, ethnic, proper, prim, elegant, interesting, rich, soft

6

Uncovering Your Assets

To make the most of your assets you must know that they exist. But how do you begin to discover your assets when all you see in the mirror are your flaws? How do you change a negative critic into a positive helpmate? The answer: You point out all the good things that are being ignored. If you do not believe that you have any assets, you simply do not know where to look.

Everyone has assets. In the Introduction to this book I promised that each person has at least five, and you will discover that you have many more. The trick is to look at yourself as a well-designed package, and uncover the special beauty that is unique to you. If you take your body apart piece by piece and measure it against a fashion model's, it is bound to look imperfect. I clearly remember being sixteen years old and tacking a picture of Cheryl Tiegs to my closet door. "If I lose a little weight," I thought to myself, "my waist will go in just like hers."

Well, I was wrong. But in its own way, my waistline is fine, and I am conscious of choosing clothes that flatter it. That was not always the case, however;

for years I hid it as best I could. Reading that a woman's waist should always measure ten inches less then her hips and bust convinced me my waist was too big, just as I am certain that photographs of today's models have undermined any appreciation you might otherwise have felt for yourself.

There are certain parts of a woman's body that are assets no matter what they measure. Before I take a new client shopping, I take note of the assets I want to be sure to focus on. Without exception, there are three areas that automatically go on the list: her face, breasts, and the overall look of her body. Usually, much to my clients surprise, many ill-thought-of physical attributes also make the list.

Assets do not always announce themselves; they need to be sought out. Follow my directions of where and how to look, and I am certain you will find them.

Starting at the top, the focal point of the picture you are creating is always your *face*. When you were describing aspects of your physical self in the previous chapter, you should have identified areas that you like. Did you find you have positive feelings about your eyes, your nose, your dimples, or your coloring? Your face is your foremost asset, so when you are selecting clothes, you should always be aware of framing it in flattering way. Your smile, your sparkle, and your expressiveness need only to be enhanced by their surroundings.

An aspect of your *neck*, *shoulders*, or *chest*, which play a supporting role in focusing attention on your face, can be an asset. Do you have a long or graceful neck? Are your shoulders delicate, straight, strong, or broad? Is your upper chest highlighted by striking collarbones with distinctive ridges and hollows? Is the skin on your chest and shoulders smooth and creamy? Whatever your best features are in this area of your body, be sure they are not eclipsed, or the beauty of your face will not be displayed to its fullest advantage. Choose a flattering neckline to enhance both your face and the assets of your upper body.

The shape of your shoulders, neck, and chest indicate your overall bone structure, so it is important to work with them, not against them. I always hated my scrawny "bird" shoulders, especially since with my full breasts they were always too narrow for blouses to fit properly. One day I realized my shoulders, when considered with my graceful neck and tapering fingers, were all part of a delicate and elegant bone structure. Soon after my revelation I discovered it did not matter that I was unable to wear blouses with set-in sleeves that buttoned up the front, because there were many other styles of sweaters and shirts that showed off both my delicate bones and full breasts. If you are unable to see your neck and shoulders in a positive light, remember they reflect your bone structure, which determines to a large degree the overall shape of your body.

This brings us to another feature that is always an asset, and that is the overall look of your body. It is crucial that you stop taking yourself apart, so you can step back and get an overview. No matter what shape it is in, every person's body structure is an asset that needs to be enhanced. This may be a difficult concept to grasp at first, but if you work with the lines nature has drawn you will be able to create a complimentary picture. For example, if you are short and feel somewhat stocky, there is a compactness about you. If clothing fits well and stays close to your body, you will look compact and sleek. Even if you are not as slim as you would like to be, if you are solid or muscular you can focus on the strength and dynamic energy of your body. If you are one of the many women with a small torso and curvy, full hips, treating your feminine shape as an asset will enable you to look both gracious and graceful. Focus on appreciating your overall look.

As you continue your search for assets, move farther down your body to your *breasts*. Every woman's breasts are an asset. Small, large, or in-between, they are an essential part of a woman's beauty and femininity. Our culture has convinced us to believe otherwise by telling us that "medium"

I basically think my body is okay as a whole total. It's not that I wouldn't want to change it, but overall I like it just the way it is. I can't separate out one part from another because it is all part of who I am. I concentrate on buying clothes that make the total package look good.

Debbie

is the only size of breasts to be proud of (unless you want to model for *Playboy*, then the bigger the better).

Consider the absurdity of this for a moment. Full-breasted women feel awkward. Small-breasted women feel inadequate. Historically, fashion has dictated popular breast dimensions, but women continue to develop in all shapes and sizes.

I consider a woman's breasts to be one of her best features, because framed in a flattering way they always are. If you feel your breasts are too large or too small for the clothes you have been trying on, then you have yet to discover the ideal style. If you are voluptuous, you know that certain outfits can make you appear overstuffed and matronly. Draped by a different garment, however, your breasts will look sensuous, curvy, and lovely. Their shape helps to bring a garment to life. If you are not generously endowed, you may feel skinny or "flat as a washboard," but the right style will show off your size to their best advantage. The most important thing is to think of your breasts in a positive light. No matter what your size, don't camouflage or ignore them: treat them like the assets they are.

The *waistline* is another wonderfully feminine area that most women feel inadequate about. It does not have to be a tiny nineteen inches (or twenty-five for that matter) to be an asset. Unless you have absolutely no curve at the waist at all, it is an area to emphasize. The trick is once again knowing what belt or style will best flatter it, and that depends upon the shape of your midriff, tummy, and hips. Even if your waist looks wide to you, don't discount its potential.

Your *midriff*, the area beneath your breasts and above your waistline, may be slender and shapely even if your waistline is not. Your entire upper torso could be an asset that is being overlooked. Whether you are long waisted or short waisted, take advantage of every feminine curve you have.

The shape of their hips is a source of displeasure and frustration for many women. "Too wide, too fat, too curvy," goes the lament, "too big for pants, a nightmare when trying to find clothes." Others bemoan their narrow hips and flat rear end. The loathing I have seen directed towards hips and thighs surpasses any other area of the body. They are usually simple to camouflage with a soft skirt, but the opportunity to show off a generous backside should not be overlooked. Hips can look too wide in one outfit and gloriously shapely in the next. Unless you consider the possibility that your *hips* could be an asset, they will always appear offensive to you. Don't always assume that just because the curve of your hips shows, it therefore looks unattractive.

I always used to feel my rear end was too big. I have had a lot of compliments from men all my life, but I didn't believe them. So I am believing them now. They're right!

Gloria

If you are lucky enough to have a pretty back, make the most of it whenever possible. The new bra styles allow you to show off more then ever before and still receive support if you need it.

You probably have a fairly realistic appraisal of your *legs*. If you like them, show them off! If they are less than perfect, you can still choose styles that flatter them as much as possible. For some reason, legs seem less vulnerable to intense self-criticism. Make the most of your legs with the shoes, hosiery, and hemlines you choose.

Do not forget that your *hands*, *feet*, *wrists*, and *ankles* can all be considered assets. Pay attention to what flatters them. No area is too small or insignificant for you to appreciate, especially at first. Seeing any aspect of yourself in a kindly way opens the door to new positive self-discoveries. Concentrate on what you like now, and watch for areas to add to your assets list.

What I have been attempting to get across during this bodily run down is that for an area to look like an asset, it must first be considered one. If you don't expect a part of you to look good, it never will. You will keep gravitating to the same familiar camouflaging styles time and again, and feel frustrated that nothing ever looks great.

When I take clients shopping, they are often astounded to discover they have a nice waistline or a shapely bottom. It is a gratifying experience to discover that an area, once considered a flaw, can now be an asset. The primary difference between what I am able to do for my clients and what they are able to do for themselves is that I am looking for their assets. I am always alert to an area that needs some creative camouflage, but my efforts never stop there. I know that the secret to helping my clients look wonderful is to make the most of their assets, and I can hardly wait to go shopping so I can prove it to them.

Your ultimate goal is to choose clothing that will flatter your entire body. In order to do that successfully, you need to see your overall shape in a positive, yet realistic, way. If years of feeling inadequate or imperfect have left you unable to be objective, the first step is to concentrate on finding things about yourself that you like. There will be a period of time when you will have to ask yourself if the specific area you have identified as an asset is being flattered. When you gaze into a dressing room mirror, the crucial question will be: "Does this outfit show off my best features?" When you see that consciously making the most of your assets improves your overall appearance, you will discover that you have more going for you than you previously had thought. When you replace the never satisfied critic with a positive frame of mind, you will then be able to tell at a glance if a garment is showing off your face and figure to their best advantage.

Over time, the process of liking how you look will become more automatic and unconscious, but at first it takes a concerted effort. Feeling momentarily uplifted or inspired by what you have just read is not enough. There are too many opposing messages coming from all directions that will cause you to doubt yourself. It is extremely helpful to make a list of your assets, just like the list you compiled on your fashion spirit. Use emotionally descriptive adjectives like "strong" shoulders, "smooth" back, "shapely" legs, "elegant" hands, or "delicate" breasts to help clarify why you consider them assets. If you are unclear about what your assets are, at least make a commitment to discover some pluses.

Looking at your naked body is not necessarily the most revealing place to begin. It is too familiar and too difficult to focus on objectively. Use clothing to help you find areas to appreciate. Watch for something that looks good on all or part of you, and then figure out why. If you like something about a garment, but it doesn't fit your body, budget, or lifestyle perfectly, take note of what area the style is enhancing. Shopping can be a time for learning and observation. For example, in recent years dropped-waist dresses have come into fashion. If they look good on you, you can assume that a long, shapely torso is one of your assets. On the other hand, if your waist curves in and your hips or tummy immediately curve out, when you try on a drop-waisted garment, you will incorrectly assume you are too heavy or hippy. Disregard this style in favor of a skirt or dress that defines the natural waistline, and watch your shape return to a more pleasing outline.

Take notice of the wonders the right belt can do for your feminine figure. Many women who are convinced they have no waistline are astonished at the definition a wide belt can provide. If you know you look better in a straight skirt and jean-style pant than in a full skirt or pleated trouser, then your slim or straight hips are an asset. A belt worn low on the hips or a fanny-wrap might be a good style for you.

Watch to see what neckline, waistline, and hemline flatter your proportions. If you are swallowed up by a long or voluminous garment, your petite stature or compact shape may be, rather than a fashion liability, an asset waiting to be enhanced.

Once you have a list of your assets, what do you do with it? First of all, add to it. Second, use it. Refer to it often. Before you venture into the stores read it over, and read it again at the end of a discouraging expedition. It is up to you to reinforce the idea that you have wonderful attributes worth emphasizing. The styles, the models, the salespeople, and the displays will all attack your confidence and activate your fears about not measuring up. Fight back by

I like my nose, I have a great smile and great twinkly eyes. I think the bones in my neck are pretty; I have a nice waist, and great long legs.

Debbie

continuing to think positively. Just keep in mind that it does not have to be the current standard of ideal beauty to be an asset. Remind yourself that improving or changing how you look is not the solution. No matter how many pounds you were to lose or muscles you were to tone, you would still have to discover your assets and make the most of them.

If you believe that you can look good, you will. You will wait to see something wonderful in the mirror, and hold off buying anything until you do. You will love the clothes that bring out the best in you, and pretty soon you will love *you*. When the fashions don't work it will be the clothes you hate, not yourself. Knowing that clothes can look great on you will give you the energy to persevere until you find that special something that is exactly right.

When you develop a conscious awareness of your assets, you are arming yourself with extra information that will make the search for clothing indescribably simpler. By formulating an idea of your spirit and your assets, you will be able to tell at a glance if an item is worth considering. Gone forever will be the days of trying on outfit after outfit, puzzled as to why nothing looks right, and not knowing what to do to make it better.

7

Your Colors: Beyond Swatches and Seasons

Your "colors" are not simply little swatches that you carry around with you and attempt to match up to clothing. In its purest form, color is light energy, and the essence of that energy should match your own inner vitality. The colors you choose to wear are the richest form of self-expression available to you. To fully experience Clothing Your Spirit, your sense of color must be a part of the process.

Surrounding yourself with the colors that are right for you is like falling in love: it reaches right to the core of your being. When you gaze at color it wings its way directly past your critical judgment faculties. So much is made of the use of color in fashion because it magically transforms something as mundane as a collection of fabric, zippers, and seams into a vehicle for the enhancement of beauty. We all want the colors we wear to flatter us, and much has been made about the best colors to accomplish this. In keeping with the philosophy of Clothe Your Spirit, "your colors" are those that express your inner essence and bring out the best of your natural beauty.

When I wear pink I feel I look like a pink cloud.
Gloria

I am very attracted to the light pinks and violets—amethyst, pink, purple, periwinkle, rose, and berry shades. I used to gravitate to the earth tones to help me feel more grounded, but now that I feel more grounded within myself, I am able to wear these colors and express my essence more freely.
Serita

When I look back at my wardrobe, it felt drab and I felt drab. Now I feel much brighter and sunnier. I was choosing colors that were "in," and not necessarily colors that suited me. I feel so good in my new colors, so springy.
Gloria

You can learn how to channel your emotional responses toward color into the intuition you are developing about yourself. Earlier you were asked to determine some terms that best described your spirit in relationship to fashion. Much of what you learned about yourself during the exploration of your spirit can be applied to color. As you recall, the words I chose to describe my spirit were sophisticated, straightforward, sensuous, and sparkling. Like anything else, color has a "feel" to it. I might look fine in fire-engine red, but it would not "feel" as good to me as a red the color of claret wine. The richer, deeper tone evokes a more sensuous and sophisticated quality.

Many of the terms I listed to describe one's spirit also apply to color—words like intense, vivid, gentle, soft, rich, earthy, clear, fresh, cheerful, sunny, and vibrant. Consider the words you chose for yourself. What colors do they immediately bring to mind? As you continue to explore the adjectives that describe your spirit, look to the qualities of the colors you prefer to provide you with further clues.

Looking at color beyond how it simply looks on you is an integral part of the relationship between your inner and outer self. You want your clothes to tell something about you to all those you come into contact with. People are going to react to the color you have on, and if the color is an expression of your spirit, they will be drawn to both the color and to you.

I was recently asked to speak at a gathering of professional women, and as I was waiting to go on I looked around the room, taking in the people and my surroundings. A deep-purple suit, worn with a striking black blouse, caught my eye. On top of the suit was the timid face of a blond-haired, fair-complected young woman, looking uncomfortable as she stood slightly apart from the group. I knew she had chosen the dashing outfit to give her confidence and to make her feel bold, but it did not appear to be working. As I gazed at her, I was conscious of the "off" quality of the image she was presenting. I imagined her beauty enhanced by a fuzzy angora sweater dress in a delicate shade of the softest lavender. Her shyness and vulnerability would have been apparent for everyone to see, and it is likely that the group would have done more to make her feel welcome.

Too much color is like a force field: it repels rather than attracts. Yet on a vibrant person, too subtle a color fades away into the background. I could easily imagine the purple suit on Debbie, with her black hair, her snapping black eyes, and her laugh that can always be heard across a crowded room. The intense color would be a good match for Debbie's energy, and the picture she presented would have attracted women that wanted to take part in her high spirits. The key is for you to wear the amount of color that is right for you, never allowing the color to dominate.

The combination of colors that you wear is every bit as important as any single color you choose. Colors play off each other, and the harmonious way they blend or contrast makes a statement. If the purple suit described above was worn with a blouse in lilac instead of black, the impact would have been quite different. A subtle combination can make a color come across in a whole new way. Black and white are often chosen indiscriminately as basics, but when worn with other colors they create distinct contrasts. Black and white are not really colors, but "impact makers." Their look is dramatic, which is primarily why people choose them. Drama is fashionable and fun, but be careful of relying too heavily on black and white, lest they limit your full range of expression. Because they lack pigment, black and white can be harsh colors to wear. Black might be all you crave for a night out, or white the only color that appeals to you during the heat of summer, but let an honest look in the mirror tell you if they are truly flattering.

To make the most of your inner spirit and your physical assets, you need to choose colors that enhance and support your unique beauty. Your foremost asset is your face, so the single greatest factor influencing how you look is the color that surrounds it. Color enhances your beauty by heightening your natural coloring. Observe what shades make your eyes stand out and sparkle. Wearing the same red as the natural red in your lips and cheeks makes your skin glow. Do you feel the most attractive in pure red, or do you prefer a rose, peach, or burgundy tone? Playing up the assets on your face (eyes, lips, cheeks) causes the areas we want to camouflage (wrinkles, lines, blemishes) to naturally recede. When you wear one of your great colors, you can not help but notice how attractive you are. When you look in the mirror, your best features shine through. When you are selecting clothes, be sure the colors are doing all they can for you. Notice what colors make you feel drab or pale. Do others help you feel alive and healthy, soft and feminine, dashing and dramatic? Pay attention to both the colors you feel the best in and the colors you are drawn to.

I wish I could tell you to turn to the end of the chapter and do exercises to help you determine what your range of best colors are. Unfortunately, I can not. I originally wrote pages of instructions that, although they made perfect sense to me, could too easily be open to misinterpretation. It is better to trust what you see for yourself in the mirror than attempt to understand written advice and make incorrect assumptions.

Professional color analysis is another option. The field of color analysis has been developing since the 1940's, and in its current state it has both benefits and pitfalls. It is an important responsibility to tell someone what colors they should or should not wear. We are so vulnerable when it comes to our appearance, so anxious to do what is right, that a supposed "authority" can have a significant impact. Having your colors done is probably not an experience you can take lightly. It can confirm your instincts about color, or it can deny them. It can expand your world by adding new colors you love, or it can make you feel guilty about wearing colors

I get these little freckles in the summer time, which fade away in the winter. In the summer I used to feel like hiding, I didn't like my freckles at all. But now, with all the bright colors I have been wearing, they don't look too bad; they kind of match the clothes I am wearing.

Holly

you formerly enjoyed but do not appear on your color chart. The real drawback in packaging color into little books of swatches is that it plays on the fear of doing wrong. Beware of allowing the emphasis on "good" and "bad" colors to spoil your enjoyment of color.

At its best, color analysis can be truly life enhancing. At its worst, it can send you off in the totally wrong direction. When it is done well, it provides a reflection of your inner energy and an enhancement of your natural beauty. The effect of wearing colors that reflect your spirit can be magical. It has made a dramatic impact on me, and on many of the people I have worked with. The critical thing to remember when working with any image professional is to not leave your instincts at the door. The longer you work with Clothe Your Spirit, the stronger your sense of what is right for you will grow.

The value of an image consultant is that he or she can look through some of your barriers, clearly see your beauty, and explain how to best show it off. A well-trained color analyst has spent months studying color theory and is highly skilled at identifying human color patterns and harmonies. But only you can know if what you are being told is in alignment with your spirit. What he or she says must ring true. If someone has done your colors in the past, and it has never felt right to you, it probably isn't. When I finish doing a color palette for individuals, they often tell me, "This feels like me." If you have your colors done and are not pleased with the results at first, give the palette a chance. If you continue to feel uneasy, or uncomfortable with it, then something is wrong. Your colors should feel good, exactly right for you. When you wear your colors, you should be astonished and delighted by how good you look. Your shopping and wardrobe-building process should be greatly simplified. The entire experience should be positive and satisfying. If it is not, then chalk it up to trial and error, and discard the information in the same way you would cast off a mistaken purchase. At least twenty-five percent of my

I knew they were the perfect colors as soon as I saw them. I was so excited. The colors you gave me were intense, but rich intense. I always carry them around and I always use them. I want to find clothes in those colors because I like them and they make me feel good.
Debbie

clientele have already had their colors done elsewhere and were not satisfied with the results. Color analysis is an unregulated industry, and there are bound to be people who hang out a shingle without fully understanding the nature of what they are doing. I can't tell you which color analysts are the best, but in Chapter Thirteen "Finding Help" I offer tips for choosing an image consultant.

Whether you decide to work with a color consultant or chose to experiment with color on your own, your involvement with color is what counts. You do not have to have your colors done professionally in order to experience the excitement and emotional impact color can provide. Your experience of color is not limited to liking how you look. When you open your senses, the pleasures of color make one delight at being alive. I use the colors of my clothes and my surroundings to nourish and satisfy me. While reviewing my notes on color, I came upon this journal entry written last winter:

"The day is dark, drizzly, and cold. My grey flannel slacks, teal silk blouse, and thick purple sweater make me feel better, for the sheer comfort of the color alone. Looking at color on other people also gives me a lift. I run into Katharine, and, in her violet sweater and clear pink turtleneck, she is a pleasing oasis of springlike loveliness and vitality. As I sit drinking my coffee I notice a young woman seated nearby, dressed in red tights, a blue jean mini-skirt, and a sweater patterned with bright red, yellow, and blue geometrics. Outside a woman walks by in a purple warm-up suit, white raincoat, and purple umbrella. I hope that her colors make her feel as good as I do looking at her."

Look at color! It is everywhere around you—in nature, in art, on signs, billboards, buildings, and on other people. Your ability to discriminate between variations of hue, tone, shade, and intensity will improve with practice. Your emotional response to color will also develop with use. Clothe Your Spirit helps you to turn inward, to respond to your emotions, to develop a sense of what is right for you. You will be delighted to discover how quickly your feeling for color will grow. As you become more sensitive to the subtleties and variations within the spectrum, your appreciation for the uniqueness of your own coloring will flourish. Opening yourself up to all the options, and then allowing yourself to be drawn to what feels right for you, will once again help you to streamline your choices and simplify your wardrobe building.

Let color make your day. Let it lift your mood, broaden your expression, and refresh you when you feel your old look has grown tiresome. The colors that look the best on you are one more aspect of your unique spirit. Explore, experience, and enjoy them.

8

Lifestyle: Making Your Clothes Work For You

Visualize yourself at a social gathering filled with old friends and new aquaintances. You are clothed in something festive, neither terribly casual nor dressy. During this visualization focus on how you feel rather than on the specifics of your clothing. As you look around the room at the other guests you see you have chosen your outfit perfectly and are dressed in an ideal fashion. Your look is "on the button" for both the mood and occasion.

When you left home, your final glance in the mirror assured you that you looked great, terrific in fact. A glow of confidence enveloped you, combined with a twinge of excitement about the reactions you might receive. As you arrive at your destination you know you still look as good as when you left, because you avoided anything that would be crushed or wrinkled in transit. The only necessary adjustments to your outfit are minor ones, nothing annoying like fabric bunching up around a belt or a slippery scarf that refuses to stay put. Everything is comfortable and non-constrictive, with plenty of latitude for dancing or eating. Your feet will last all night in their soft leather shoes—no pinching or tottery high heels allowed!

You look your best, and you feel comfortable and appropriate. You can forget your appearance, your clothes, and have a grand time.

Too much to ask for?

Not at all!

It is important and necessary to ask for "too much" rather than too little. Feeling satisfied with your wardrobe is determined by how well your clothing fits your needs. The clearer you can be about exactly what you need your clothes to do for you, the better. If you suffer from the closet-full-of-clothes-but-nothing-to-wear syndrome, you need to take a closer look at your lifestyle. A packed closet can leave you unfulfilled and hungry for more if the clothes are not ideally suited to the occasions you need them for. It does not take many clothes to feel fulfilled; it takes having the right ones.

Stop and take the time to consider your lifestyle. This includes a careful breakdown of how you spend your time, what physical requirements you have of your clothing, and the amount of maintenance and upkeep you are willing to undertake. Exercises at the end of the chapter will help you focus specifically on these areas.

Clarifying your needs will help you to narrow your options and assist you in making satisfying choices. It is a natural reaction to gravitate towards types of clothing and styles that you like and that look well on you, but chances are you do not need to duplicate things you already own. Consciously focusing on your needs will help you to move in a more appropriate direction.

Do not be afraid of asking for too much. I ask my clients to focus on exactly what they want from their clothes before we go shopping. I have heard some difficult requests that seem nearly impossible at the time, but somehow we always manage to fulfill them. In fact, it frequently proves to be helpful by defining our search. Being wide open to every option is not necessarily desirable.

When I used to get dressed there was a lot of homogeneity associated with it. My wardrobe looked essentially the same. I had twelve Paul Stanley gabardine suits. The thing that I enjoyed most about getting dressed then was wearing the clothes that had just come from the cleaners. The excitement was that they were clean and pressed. I didn't really have any clothes for getting dressed up and going out, or casual wear.

Serita

How do you really spend your time? Recently I was in an exclusive men's clothing store, helping a gentleman select a sportscoat. The salesperson said to him, "If you turn the collar up and wear the coat with a sweater, it would be perfect for a weekend in the country with friends." I turned to my client and said, "I don't spend weekends in the country. Do you?" I knew exactly what he needed the sportcoat for, and I was not at all surprised to hear his negative reply. It brought us right back to reality and the fact that this particular coat, while very attractive, did not fulfill the need for which it was intended.

The glamour of the suggested "weekend in the country" was very appealing, but not realistic. It is fun to daydream about exciting uses for an outfit, but if they are not part of your activities, then don't get caught up in a salesperson's fantasy.

Choosing clothes for the Christmas season is an especially good time to focus on being realistic. Every year the glamorous, glittery clothing catches my eye, but the biggest event of my holidays is serving chili and sandwiches at my New Year's Day Open House. If your office party consists of a lunchtime potluck, and Christmas Day finds you relaxing with your family, then select an outfit that is both festive and appropriately casual. It is equally important for you to feel wonderful whether you are at an extravaganza or spending a quiet evening with friends. Your own occasions are as special as anything in the society pages.

Special occasions are the spice of life, but if money is a consideration, "special occasion" clothes should take up only a small portion of your total wardrobe. Your clothing needs for your day-to-day activities require the most consideration. If you work, you do more than just go to the office and come home. All the different roles and tasks your job requires should be examined. And what about after work?

What you do does not have to be dazzling to be considered a social life. A nearly universal complaint from the working women that I meet is their lack of pretty weekend and casual wear. Once the shortage

Every special occasion was always a mad scramble to get something new. I'd wait until the last minute and get discouraged and fall back on something I already had or get an accessory to make it feel new. Now I can go into my closet and think, "Oh, I can put this or that together." I wore the suit I got for job interviews to a wedding and I felt just perfect.
Gloria

in that area is duly noted, it is easy and relatively inexpensive to fill the gap.

Nothing that you do is too insignificant to be considered. If you are at home with the kids most the day, but meet a friend for lunch or run errands in the afternoon, your clothes need to have both the durability for the children's abuse and the appropriate "out-of-the-house" polish. None of us has the time or inclination to be constantly thinking about clothes. My current priority is being warm and cozy while I spend the day writing, but I do not want to change if I decide to go out later. It is also necessary for me to feel good while spending long, lonely hours at my desk. Feeling good about how you look even when no one else sees you is part of Clothing Your Spirit.

In a previous chapter, I discussed the importance of knowing what your assets are and making the most of them. It will not do for your assets to be in evidence some of the time and eclipsed during others. For you to believe in yourself and your own beauty, you need to be reinforced every time you look in the mirror. You look in the mirror when you are home alone, and on evenings and weekends, too. For your own sense of pride and confidence, you need to like what you see.

Next, consider the physical requirements you have of your clothing. Clothing was originally designed as protection from the elements, and those needs are just as relevant today. Being inside a building may protect us from the blazing heat of the sun, but what about the chill of an air conditioner? Our technology has advanced, but so have our demands. We still have the need for comfort, protection, and decency, but we insist our clothing look attractive and communicate something about us. No matter how wonderful something looks, unless it covers us and keeps us warm and protected, it is of little use.

Comfortable clothes that fit well, that do not bind, pinch, pull, rub, or grab, are an absolute given. You should never buy or wear clothes that do any of the above; it is totally unnecessary. There are plenty of clothes that will fit easily, no matter what your size. If something becomes too tight, take it out of your closet and don't torture yourself.

I doubt there is a woman reading this book who has not become so enamored with a pair of shoes that she bought them knowing full well they would never be comfortable enough. I get annoyed with myself when I spend money foolishly, and I am sure that at some future date I will again get caught up in the golden glow of looking wonderful and buy something for its appearance alone. I avoid this as much as possible by believing I can have both beauty and comfort and refusing to settle for less.

When I am working, I spend so much time shopping and in stores that comfortable feet are a top priority. This means flat shoes, so I build many of my outfits from the ground up. Looking stylish while wearing walking shoes is a requirement of my job, so either I manage to pull it off or I spend the day feeling miserable.

What are your comfort priorities? Some people hate the itchiness of wool, the heaviness of lined pants, or the feel of polyester. A wrap skirt can be an annoying distraction in a professional situation. A blouse with a high neck can make a sensitive wearer feel constrained all day. A woman with allergies is miserable if her garment does not have a pocket for her tissue. In some areas we dress to ward off the chill, but in other areas we attempt to avoid garments that are too hot or heavy. Cool mornings and warm afternoons, air-conditioned buildings, unpredictable breezes, and the varying climates in coastal areas all demand coordinating layers. Keeping in mind your priorities for comfort will help you avoid buying clothes you do not enjoy or that just hang in your closet.

The next physical requirement you have of your clothes is their wearability, including how they stand up to use and the amount of maintenance they require. If you love the crispness of freshly ironed linen but hate how it looks when it becomes a mass of wrinkles, then maybe it is not a fabric for you.

Crushable natural fibers are not for everyone, especially those who feel "frumpy" in clothes that lose their shape and sleekness. Sending a garment to the cleaners after every wearing is not an acceptable solution for most people. You have a right to expect a reasonable amount of durability from your clothes. If you avoid wearing clothes because you dislike the required upkeep, then stay away from that type of garment in the future. A beautiful silk blouse is not much good gracing a hanger.

I have a friend who lives on a houseboat with two small children. When we were shopping together several years ago she told me that she did not intend to buy anything that needed to be dry cleaned or ironed. Since seventy-five percent of my clothing requires both, I wondered what she would select. She ended up with a short leather skirt, a wide jersey circle skirt, boots, and coordinating washable sweaters and t-shirts. I was impressed. Later a client asked my help with selecting a wardrobe for a European trip that was to begin during the warmth of late summer and continue through mid-winter. I assured her that finding durable, lightweight clothes that could be layered and would not become badly wrinkled was the solution and was indeed possible. The clothes we found fully expressed her spirit, and no compromise of practicality was necessary.

You should ask for everything you want, even if it seems like you are being overly picky. You will be pleasantly surprised to discover that being clear about what you want actually makes shopping easier. Instead of feeling limited, you will find that awareness throws open the doors to new options.

In the following chapter, you will be going through your closet and looking at the clothes you currently own. Keep in mind your lifestyle considerations when you are evaluating the usefulness of each garment. You may discover the clothing you do own is woefully unrelated to what you actually do with your time. If this is the case, do not despair. It is an easy pattern to fall into when certain kinds of clothing look good on you. Once you are aware of

Sometimes I buy something just to fill a functional need. I bought four trumpet skirts made from raw silk. They are swishy and comfortable and don't wrinkle. I find a fabric and a style that I love, and I stick with it.

Serita

The skirts I own now fit my lifestyle perfectly. I can dress them up by putting a nice blouse with them, or I can dress them down by wearing a t-shirt, and still have fun with them.

Holly

the problem, you can avoid continuing to duplicate what you already own and fill in where necessary. It is much easier and less costly than starting from scratch.

The following exercises will help you look even more closely at your lifestyle. Exercise One asks you to examine how you spend your time and to look at the kinds of clothes you need for your various activities. Exercise Two helps you to take note of obvious gaps in your wardrobe. Exercise Three asks you to consider your physical requirements and the final exercise helps you visualize the perfect outfit.

You will get the most out of these exercises by doing them in writing. If you do not wish to, be sure to read them over and let your mind go to work.

EXERCISE ONE:
HOW DO YOU SPEND YOUR TIME?

1. Begin by making a list of all the things you do regularly and occasionally. Structure it any way you like. One format is to make separate categories for weekdays, weekends, evenings, and special events. Other categories include work, social gatherings, entertaining, cultural events, outings, family activities, exercise, sports, vacations, and meetings. Don't neglect the little things like "Parents' Night" at your child's school.

2. After you have listed every activity you can think of, take a clean piece of paper and draw a large circle. Title this circle "Lifestyle Pie." Estimate how much time you spend on each area, and draw a pie graph representing the way your time is utilized. This graph will change, so be sure to update it regularly.

3. Draw a second pie graph, this time substituting the kind of clothes needed for each activity. Title this one "Clothes Needed." These clothing categories might include professional, very casual, dressy casual, and formal. (You will probably notice quite a bit

of overlap. This should indicate to you that buying an outfit in the "dressy casual" category would fulfill a whole range of needs. Try to buy an outfit that serves more than one function. For example, a suit needed for making presentations at work could also be worn to occasional evenings at the theatre.)

EXERCISE TWO:
ARE THERE GAPS IN YOUR WARDROBE?

1. List anything you wear repeatedly but do not like, such as a tired raincoat or an out-of-style skirt. This indicates a definite need you should attempt to fulfill with something more suitable.

2. Make a list of all the occasions for which you feel you never have the right thing to wear. This will help you further clarify the areas you need to concentrate on.

EXERCISE THREE:
CONSIDER YOUR PHYSICAL
REQUIREMENTS

1. Consider the physical requirements you have for each season. Autumn is often warm, but the whites and bright colors of summer can feel inappropriate. Perhaps lightweight clothing in more subtle colors would be a useful acquisition. If all your favorite cold-weather outfits look ghastly with rain or snow boots, your winter could be a long one. Spring makes one long for fresh, vibrant colors, but be careful if cool weather persists in your area. This year, take a positive approach to the dreaded bareness of summer dressing. If you feel uneasy about exposing your thighs, see if you can come up with a comfortable and creative substitute.

EXERCISE FOUR:
VISUALIZE THE PERFECT OUTFIT

1. This final exercise is a powerful one. Think of a

forthcoming occasion for which you want to look your absolute best. Close your eyes and visualize yourself there. What would be the perfect outfit? In specific detail, take note of what you are wearing. Perhaps it is something you have never worn before, like a backless sweater dress, or something unexpected like a jumpsuit. Let your mind wander past the traditional alternatives. (It is amazing how often I have done this only to find nearly the exact item in a store days later. I do this every time I intend to buy something new to fulfill a specific need. It works!)

PART THREE

Planning and Implementing Your Ideal Wardrobe

Debbie: Impish, Sophisticated, Dramatic, Sleek

I always thought owning clothes was an extension of who I was, so the more clothes I had, the better I was.

If I was going into a situation where I felt uncomfortable, I always wanted my clothes to protect me. Now I feel my clothes tell people something about me, even if I am in jeans and a sweatshirt.

When I first put on this outfit I knew, after all my searching, that this was it, this was the real me.

Holly: Fun, Fresh, Girlish

I thought this was a professional look. But I felt drab; I knew these clothes didn't do anything for me.

I want people to look at me and think, "This girl knows how to play!"

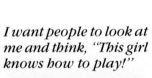

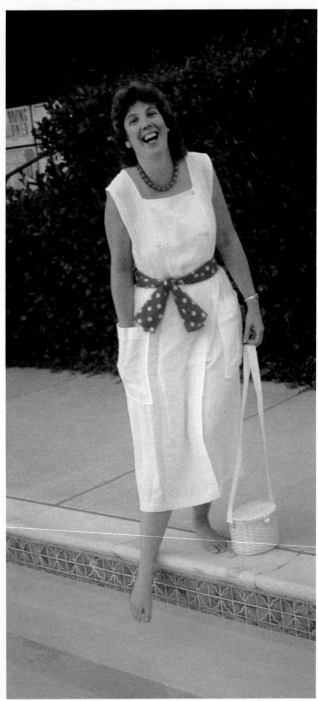

I feel confident now; I feel good about myself. I have started talking to people I never talked to before and giving my opinions at meetings.

Karen: Strong, Reserved, Informal

I no longer need such a stuffy business look.

I never would have thought about wearing clothes like this, but I love them. They feel comfortable and re-laxed. I find myself wanting to stand taller. Whenever I walk into a room, I feel confident about the way I am dressed.

Patty: Intense, Warm, Rooted

My clothes say "suburbia." My lifestyle is casual, but I would like to look more sophisticated.

I can see what a difference it makes to wear clothes that focus attention on my face.

Christy: Natural, Straightforward, Spirited

I want to look natural and informal, but at the same time professional. I am also tired of waiting to lose my extra pregnancy weight.

I brought my wardrobe into the present, and it feels great not to have to spend time worrying about it.

Loie: Fun, Daring, Dramatic

I am tired of looking like a prep. These clothes allow my more adventurous side to come through.

Marilyn: Vibrant, Vital, Free-flowing

In traditional clothing I feel like a cardboard cutout.

I have always been a free spirit, and now I feel like I am really expressing my true self.

Serita: Romantic, Feminine, Classic

My clothes all looked exactly alike. I had twelve wool gabardine suits, all in dark colors.

I feel softer, more lovable, more hugable, more frivolous, and more accepting.

I feel differently about myself. I am lighter, brighter, happier.

Gloria: Classic, Gentle, Glowing, Sunny

My self-confidence and self-esteem were so low. I didn't know where to start.

I started to think there were other things to do in life besides be drab and hide and be insecure.

I can't believe I have teenaged grandchildren when I look at myself in these pictures. It's fun to be able to play with the kids and feel like a kid and not feel like I have to dress my so-called age.

*Jennifer: Straightforward, Sophisticated,
Sensuous, Sparkling*

9

Your Closet: Getting Rid of the Skeletons

I love helping people clean out their closets. It helps me to understand their spirit and their barriers by seeing what they have collected, and I find it satisfying to make order out of chaos. I perch on the bed, feeling very authoritative as garments are displayed before me. The first few outfits I comment upon, declaring either "Looks great!" or "Get rid of it!" After my first few pronouncements, I find myself saying little else. Once into the swing of things, the intrepid closet owner begins decisively weeding out garments single-handedly. "I never liked this!" she cries. "Why have I been hanging onto this?" she exclaims, tossing it aside. I lean against the headboard and watch the discard pile grow. Earlier in the day, this vanquisher of closet clutter was fearful about our cleaning appointment. Would I be abrasive? Would she be embarrassed? Would she have to give away things she loved? What would be left to wear?

Fear might keep her from getting started, but with a little encouragement I have seen nearly everyone throw themselves into the task with gleeful abandon.

I thought it was wonderful to throw out all those clothes. I felt like a little moth coming out of its cocoon and I knew I was going to be a butterfly when it was all over. Getting rid of the clothes began to make me feel like that; I knew all those clothes were just a bunch of stuff covering up the real thing.

Debbie

Serita commented: "When we were going through my closet, I had two reactions: 'shock' and 'hallelujah.' Then I realized you have to tear down an old building before you can put a new building in its place. It is called 'constructive destruction.' "

The reason I enjoy cleaning out closets so much is because it is such an utterly positive thing to do. The state of your closet is more related to your attitude than it is to your general untidiness. When you Clothe Your Spirit, you need to consider everything in the present time, from the shape of your body to the needs of your lifestyle. Your closet must be a reflection of your commitment to the present. The only items hanging in it should be things you like and feel good in. Not only should your closet contain only current favorites, but they should be arranged in a way that you know what is available to you. In the Clothe Your Spirit process, updating and organizing your closet is important; don't skip it.

A voluminously stuffed closet is falsely comforting. If the clothes do not look good on you or do not meet the needs of your lifestyle, then you will be faced with the daily frustration of having nothing to wear and not understanding why. Even if the next time you go shopping you are determined to buy something that expresses your spirit, adding a few new outfits to the existing clutter is not a good practice. Buying something wonderful will not make up for a closet filled with things you feel unhappy about. Reinforce the Clothe Your Spirit state of mind at every turn.

If you think all the clothes hanging in your closet that you never wear are not hurting anything, guess again. Every time you see the slacks that do not fit or the never worn dress with the price tag still on it you get a little electric shock of negative energy. The "skeletons" in your closet undermine you; they tear down your confidence. The only solution is to get rid of them.

Clothes in your closet that are too small are the most destructive skeletons of all. You might push them to the back of the closet determined not to try them on until one morning, convinced that feeling this good can only mean you are thinner, you try them on and your cheerful mood deflates like a balloon. Or late one afternoon, rushing to get ready to go out, you become so totally frustrated at nothing looking right that you put them on anyway and spend the evening feeling pinched and miserable. Even if you do not wear your clothes that are too small, every time you see them hanging in your closet you will be reminded that you are "too fat."

Take everything that does not fit you *right now* out of your closet *today*. What you do with them once they're out is not as important as the act of freeing yourself from dealing with them on a daily basis. Trying on or wearing tight clothes will not motivate you to lose weight; it will only demean you and tear down your self-esteem. If it is too painful for you to get rid of them, put them in the garage or in a second closet. If you do lose weight, you can retrieve your clothes from your hiding place, but you will probably be shocked to discover how unexciting the items you invested so much energy into really are. It might be frightening or depressing to remove garments that are too small, but once you do it you will feel amazingly good about taking such a positive step towards liking and accepting yourself the way you are, not to mention sparing yourself from the agony of how bad tight clothes look and feel.

If I have something in my closet that doesn't fit, I just don't wear it. If I know something is going to be too tight I don't even put it on. I won't torture myself.
Debbie

The second kind of "skeleton" in your closet is all the bad purchases that you have never worn. Just as wearing something too tight will not motivate you to diet, the guilt you feel when you see a mistake hanging there will not prevent you from erring again. Getting caught up in the excitment of purchasing something, only to discover that you do not really wear it, happens to everyone. There is no need to feel like a failure because of it. When you are ready to face the fact that it will never look right (or fit your spirit and your lifestyle) clear it out of your closet and make way for something better. Anything hanging in your closet that makes you feel guilty when you look at it has got to go.

Another, even more insidious form of sabotage is allowing your closet to stay in a perpetual state of disorder and confusion. It guarantees that getting dressed will be forever difficult and unrewarding. Imagine trying to paint a masterpiece with a dirty paintbrush, dried up tubes of paint, and a messy workspace. If your objective is to look wonderful in the easiest and simplest way possible, then give yourself a break by ridding yourself of the clutter and cleaning up the chaos.

When you are psychologically ready to tackle your closet, the only way to procede is to plunge right in. Set aside several hours, and be sure to have a good full-length mirror in place. Your task is to take out every single item in your closet and return only the ones that you truly like and enjoy wearing. This means you have to try them *all* on. Be honest with yourself. Is the fit flattering? Does the color make you feel healthy and alive? Have you worn it recently, and if so, did you feel good in it? Go through everything and make a decision. (Specific advice about the best approach to take will follow in the exercises.) If it is unbearably difficult to be objective, consider having someone help you. Professionals like myself will be delighted to be of service, or enlist the aid of a friend. Invite someone whose flair for fashion you have always admired, and offer to do her a favor in return. Or let her assist you one week, and you can help her the next. It is invaluable to have the advice of someone not emotionally involved with your clothes. It is also less intimidating and more fun.

Whether you choose to have help or decide to go it alone, there will be certain stumbling blocks that you should be aware of. Some items are going to be more difficult to decide about than others. The types of clothing which are the toughest to be objective about are sentimental favorites and clothes you once enjoyed that no longer look as wonderful on you as they once did. Only the most sentimental items are worth keeping. I will never part with my wedding dress, a knit suit my grandmother gave me, or my

University of Sussex t-shirt. If you feel terribly attached to something made or given with love, put it where you put your other memorabilia. Do not leave it hanging in your closet. On the other hand, there is no reason to hang onto every outfit that you ever had fun in. You can retain the memories without keeping the clothes.

Clothes can only look good in the present time. Even something you enjoyed last season may no longer suit your spirit, figure, or lifestyle. Former favorites are often more difficult to be objective about than mistakes you have always hated. I recall a client clinging to several Missoni knit outfits, telling me how wonderfully they traveled and how ideal they were on her last vacation. I pointed out how the color and fit were no longer flattering, and I asked her to think about the overall enjoyment of her next holiday if she were dressed in something less than perfect. If you love something about an outfit but it no longer does your beauty justice, mentally file away what you liked about it, and when you can, replace it.

I am sorry to say that after a certain period of time nearly every outfit starts to look dated. Take a long, hard look at some of your older "classics," especially if they were purchased more than five years ago. When you wear them, are you still clothing your present-day spirit? Without noticing, you might have already replaced them with something you like better. If so, gently remove them from your closet while you give yourself a little pat on the back for having made such a fine purchase.

Going through your closet is an excellent time for learning more about yourself. As you try things on, consider the qualities of your favorite garments. What is it about the style, cut, and color that make them so beloved? In the clothes you enjoy the most, notice which of your assets are evident. (If you need a reminder of what to look for, review Chapter Six, "Uncovering Your Assets.") Pay attention to what is wrong with the outfits you are getting rid of. I recently decided to let go of a jumpsuit that I never

I never threw anything away because I didn't know what to throw away and what to keep. Until you clarify what you want, you have to keep it all because you don't know. It's the clarifying part that's hard. If you can't do that on your own, then you should find someone to help you.

Debbie

liked because I always felt too massive in it. I assumed the oversize shoulder pads were the culprit. When I looked at it more closely I realized it was not only the shoulder pads that made the garment look top heavy, but also the combination of epaulets, breast pockets, and lapels. I have avoided this style ever since. Without guilt coloring our observations, we can learn more from our mistakes.

Clean out your closet as well as you can before your next shopping trip. After you have returned from purchasing something new, do a little closet fine-tuning. It is easier to get rid of anything you were undecided about when you have something better to replace it. You also have the added incentive of making more room for your pretty new things.

Keeping your closet in shape is an ongoing process. If you change wardrobes seasonally, go through everything before you put it away. If you did not wear an item all season long, it is unlikely you will enjoy it next year. When you take out clothing that has been stored, try everything on to be sure it still fits and that you like it.

When you are deciding upon which clothes to save or discard, do not concern yourself with the fate of a reject. Base the decision purely on your enjoyment of the garment. After you have set aside all the clothes you are ready to remove, then you can choose what to do with them. There are many positive ways in which your old outfits can be put to good use. If they are recently purchased, little worn, and still stylish, you can try to sell them at a used clothing store or consignment shop. Donating clothes to a charitable organization helps others that are less fortunate and provides you with a tax write-off. There are several women's groups that sponsor "slightly worn" sales, with the proceeds going to charity.

A creative alternative is a clothes swapping party. Invite a group of friends over and ask them to bring only their best cast-offs. I have had a number of these which have been successful for all concerned. The only requirement is to be firm about people taking only the items that look wonderful on them, lest the former rejects become future clutter in their closets.

Whatever you decide to do, remember that what happens to your old clothes after they are out of your closet is really not all that important. Try not to put too much energy into finding them a new home. They are not stray orphans in need of shelter. Beware of burdening your family members with items you feel would be "just perfect" for them. Launch your clothes into the great unknown and let your loved ones find clothes that suit their spirits.

Now that you are free of all the skeletons in your closet, it is easy to organize what is left. Set up any type of system that works for you. Some people group their clothes by color, but I prefer to arrange my clothes by category. Moving from left to right I hang my slacks, then my blouses and lightweight jackets, followed by my skirts, and finally my dresses and jumpsuits. My heavy coats are stored in the hall closet, and my sweaters, exercise wear, and lingerie are all folded in drawers. If it helps you to keep your complete outfits hanging together, then by all means arrange your closet that way. Any approach that is convenient and makes sense is fine, with the exception of alloting one quarter of your closet for the things you currently wear and three quarters of the space for all the items you do not know what to do with!

Your accessories should also be organized and easily accessible. I found it was easier to hang my scarves and belts, so I purchased an inexpensive bentwood coat/hat rack, and it works wonderfully. The top spins so it is easy to find what I am looking for. Seeing my accessories hanging in plain sight often inspires me to try something new. Accessories do not take up much room, but they need to be scanned and kept current, like all the rest of your clothes.

If I sound like a fanatic about my closet, I would have to confess it is true. I consider it one of the few positive addictions I have. I am not a compulsively neat person (the rest of my home is not especially well ordered) but I have developed an appreciation for the benefits of a perfectly organized and up-to-date closet. Getting dressed is no longer a chore now that I can clearly see all my options hanging before me, and I can feel confident knowing I need only to choose an outfit based on my mood and the weather. I never have to speculate about whether something will fit or look great that day. I have already made my evaluation during a less hurried, more objective moment.

Your experience of getting dressed in the morning sets the tone for the whole day. You owe it to yourself to make it as streamlined and positive as possible. Getting dressed is your time to look in the mirror and positively interact with yourself, confirming your attractiveness and appreciating your beauty. It is a waste to spend those few precious moments throwing garments over furniture, frantically trying to pull yourself together.

In addition to the daily benefits of an organized closet, the act of cleaning it is in itself emotionally satisfying. A surge of energy takes hold when you free yourself from an unhappy past and move forward towards a more promising future. Like any intimate relationship, we create emotional bonds with our clothing. When you act decisively you will discover a sense of relief akin to quitting a job you hated or ending a relationship that is no longer working. It is a wonderful feeling to take control by letting go of past failures and making positive choices in the present. Your closet is a great place to begin and a great place to return to whenever you feel the need to do something good for yourself.

I have found the following three exercises to be the most successful approach to tackling your closet-cleaning project. Exercise One offers tips for going through your garments one at a time. Exercise Two guides you through arranging your clothes in an orderly way. The final exercise encourages you to evaluate what you have learned and note any important observations you have made.

I like looking in my closet, it makes me feel good to know that I like it all. I can take out something I like at anytime and I don't have to try on ten things. I can just reach in and know it is going to be wonderful.

Debbie

EXERCISE ONE:
PIECE BY PIECE

(1) There is no shortcut to trying every single item on, so let's get down to it. Put on good undergarments, including stockings, if you wear them. Start with your favorite clothes. Be sure to put on all the appropriate accessories, including shoes and jewelry. Admire how nice you look in them. Let the fact that you like something you own register. Take it off, hang it up, and put it somewhere out of the way: a doorknob or shower curtain rod will do.

(2) Continuing to move from best to worse, try on everything else that is left. Make whatever you have on look as good as it possibly can. If you feel inspired and come up with a new combination, terrific.

(3) If you are not thrilled with the way something looks, put it in the discard pile. Do not start a "maybe" pile! Make a decision. Tell yourself if you change your mind you can always retrieve it later. This act of decisiveness helps you break the emotional bond with the garment in question. Once you see it in the reject pile you will probably feel relieved rather than sad. Let me repeat this very important point: Making a yes or no decision is the key to successfully cleaning out your closet.

(4) You are probably getting stuck on all the odd pieces you have been saving, hoping to find the "perfect" thing to go with them. Ask yourself if you really and truly love them. Is it worth spending the necessary time, energy, and money to find them suitable partners? If you would rather spend the money on a totally new outfit, then let them go.

(5) YOU DO NOT HAVE TO FEEL BADLY ABOUT GETTING RID OF SOMETHING THAT IS STILL "GOOD"!

(6) Box up all the rejects and get them out of the way

for now. Refer to the ideas in the above chapter when you are ready to dispose of them.

EXERCISE TWO:
ARRANGING YOUR CLOTHES

1. It is now time to put back all the clothes you have decided to keep. Before you do, make sure everything is on a plastic or padded hanger. Nothing ruins the shape of a garment faster than letting it hang on a metal hanger. If you do not own enough appropriate hangers, take a break by going out and buying some.

2. Once you have gone through all your clothes, organizing what is left is the fun part. Enjoy the feeling of order you are creating. Arrange your clothes in whatever way appeals to you. Be sure there is enough space between each hanger so your clothes do not get crushed or wrinkled.

3. Your hangers should be able to move from side to side relatively freely. If your clothes are still jammed together, making it impossible for you to see what you have, then you did not get rid of enough. Take a second look.

4. You should be able to approach your closet each day knowing you look and feel good in everything in it. If you put something on and take it off more than a couple of times, then it is probably time for it to go. Once you have done the major cleaning, it is easy to keep your closet up to date and current.

EXERCISE THREE:
OBSERVATIONS

1. When you are going through your closet, keep paper and pencil handy for jotting down any observations you make. When you discover a style that looks good, make a note to refer to before your next shopping trip. Also note the unflattering styles you

want to avoid. If you discover any new assets, add them to the list you started in Chapter Three.

(2) Now is your opportunity to complete the exercises you started in the Lifestyle Chapter, in which you examined the types of clothing you need. Now list the clothes you own that fulfill the needs you described. Use the same headings as you did for your "clothes needed" pie graph, such as "work," "casual," "social/evening," etc. Make these as personal and as specific as your lifestyle. How do your lists compare to your lifestyle and "clothes needed" pies? Are there any gaps? Do you have a tendency to buy more clothes in a certain category than you need?

(3) If a large reject pile, combined with a shortage of cash for buying something new, causes you to feel anxious about not having enough to wear, use the following exercise to try to reassure yourself. Going across the top of a page enumerate all your activity and lifestyle requirements. Under each heading list an outfit you could conceivably wear if you had to. This will help you from feeling the panic that leads to impulse buying.

A FINAL NOTE

I recognize that for many people cleaning out their closets is very difficult. If this is true for you, then only attempt to do a small amount at a time. Progress only at a rate you feel comfortable with. It is not necessary to take an all-or-nothing approach to receive the benefits.

10

Clarifying Your Image: Your Fashion Collage

If you were heading out for your next shopping trip, would you know what to look for? By now you are aware of your compelling needs, but what about your heart's desires? In the previous chapters you have been asked to think about your spirit and your assets, and to probe your lifestyle and your closet. So far you have used words to describe your spirit; now you will explore a new dimension through the use of visual images. The time has come to vividly and specifically envision your ideal clothing. By looking at examples in magazines and catalogs, you can discover how your spirit can best be expressed by what is currently available in today's fashion marketplace.

The project guaranteed to assist you in clarifying your fashion image is collecting photographs that illustrate the looks that would best suit you. This is accomplished by gathering together all the magazines and publications you can find, and then going through them looking for images that catch your eye. Scissors in hand, cut out everything that appeals to you. If you frequently purchase fashion magazines, start tearing out pictures whenever you read them and put them in a folder. If you do not look at magazines regularly, make a point of buying a selection and setting aside some time to go through them.

Not everyone is a fan of fashion magazines. It is difficult to feel any rapport with the thin models, the way-out styles, and the astronomical prices. Do not despair, because when you approach high-fashion publications with a specific purpose in mind they become much less intimidating. Think of looking at an outrageous layout in an abstract rather than literal sense. You might not want to look like any of the models, even if you could grow ten inches taller overnight, but the quality of certain photographs may appeal to you. Look at the colors, and at the mood and image created. An aspect of the look might be attractive to you—perhaps the hairstyle, hat, jewelry, or other accessories. Translating a high-fashion magazine into terms you can relate to takes a little practice, but doing so is such a useful process that it is worthwhile to give it a try.

If you want to find examples of clothing that are more realistic, there are plenty of options to choose from. Many publications make a point of displaying outfits that are less fashion-forward and more practical. Look for a good blend of contemporary and wearable. If realistic layouts are more to your liking, do not overlook the women's magazines that focus on home and family.

Catalogs are a wonderful supplement to magazines, especially since they usually show clothing you could actually go into a store and buy. Visit stores that give them away. Ask to be on their mailing list. I order the Speigel catalog every season because it is chock full of clothing and costs only a few dollars. Catalogs can usually be yours for the asking. If they arrive in the mail unsolicited, consider them a uselful tool instead of junk mail.

Keep alert to any possible source for ideas. Most big-city newspapers have a fashion section. Advertising, especially in Sunday supplements, often offers a selection of options. Your favorite special-interest magazine might have a fashion layout or an appealing ad. Wherever you look, the important thing is to take the time to develop a feel for what you like.

Once you have collected all the examples of looks you like, you need to decide what to do with them. You can start a file that you refer to before you go shopping, or you can take the benefits of your efforts even further by creating a collage. A collage is an artistic composition of images presented on a large surface. When you construct a collage you sort through all the photographs you have gathered and arrange your favorites on a poster or art board. Both the process of creating a collage and the finished product are useful tools for clarifying your fashion image. Choosing, cutting, and arranging the looks you like help you to refine the choices you originally made. Assembling the collage requires a kind of focused concentration that often stimulates new ideas. Doing any type of art-related project activates a part of the brain that, for most of us, is used infrequently.

Creating your collage allows you to bring to life the terms that you chose to describe your spirit. Apply them to the pictures and see if they fit. You also have the opportunity to observe where your spirit is right now, today, by noting the types of images you are drawn to. Your collage is a visual summary of where you are this minute, and the finished product becomes a valuable reference point. If you put together a collage seasonally, you can clearly see the direction you are moving. It is satisfying to watch a visual statement of yourself emerge and evolve.

You can enhance your collage by adding images other than clothes. Looking at a number of completed collages from my last workshop, I see the addition of flowers, textures, home furnishings, antiques, bath products, make-up and perfume, food and drink, people interacting, and scenes from nature. The creativity is wonderful! Several of the collages contain eye-catching words or phrases. A favorite of mine states, "Not all great sparklers are measured in carats." You can put anything at all on your creation as long as you do not veer away from the goal of clarifying your fashion image.

Do not let the fear that someone might laugh at your choices stand in your way. You don't have to look like the model to be drawn to what she has on. Your collage is *your* interpretation of what *you* want (and you don't have to show it to anyone). If you know a mini-skirt might not be your most flattering choice, but you like the wild, carefree quality of the look, then acknowledge what is speaking to you and go ahead and put it on your poster board. On the other hand, it is human nature to want what we don't have. Your collage should not be a fantasy based on someone else's body. Concentrate on your positive points, your uniqueness, and the qualities about yourself that you like. When you are first collecting images, don't censor anything that catches your eye. Your finished collage, however, should consist primarily of photos or sketches of clothing that both appeal to you and that you think you would look good in.

Your collage will become a vehicle for communicating with your inner spirit. Working on it will help you to clarify what you are consciously and unconsciously craving. During the last workshop that Stephanie came to, she created a collage full of beach scenes, sunsets, and crisp blue and white clothes. Every outfit was relaxed and carefree. Even the models were at ease—one leaned on an elbow, another strolled beside the shore. Although her clothing choices had always reflected the freshness and charm of her spirit, in the past Stephanie was usually drawn to more classic looks. This collage was a real departure.

"I didn't realize how much I had been longing for summer," she responded when I pointed out my observations to her. "It was a hard winter from me, full of transitions. Now I just want to relax and feel comfortable." Stephanie's collage provided us with information that was useful on our next shopping trip. The clothes we looked for were as classy and charming as ever, but a more relaxed expression was definitely needed.

At times an unclear urge will bubble up inside of you. Something is changing, and you need a way to direct the energy. My stepdaughter, Sharon, a sunny blond who dresses in peaches, pinks, and turquoise, suddenly developed a craving for black leather. When we talked about it she told me what she really wanted was to be less cute, less "bubble-gum." We both knew black leather would not make her happy for long, so I encouraged her to find some looks that included both her spirit and the need for change she was feeling. I sent her home with a stack of magazines, and when I spoke to her again she told me that she was so excited by the more sophisticated expression she was discovering that she had attached the photographs to lampshades for lack of a proper art board.

In most circumstances, a poster board available at a local art store will do just fine. You will also need scissors and rubber cement. Before you start, decide if you want your collage to be realistic, fantasy, or a combination of both. Your board has two sides that can be used for different purposes if you so desire. I usually concentrate on making the front exactly the way I want it and put my overflow on the back. When you are assembling your collage, all the elements should be in harmony. If an item looks out of place, take it off. An advantage of taking the time to assemble a collage is discovering the discordant images that do not fit in. What you find you don't like is as telling as what you do.

Even though you want your collage to be an accurate reflection of where you are, there is no need to belabor your creation. Don't get bogged down thinking it has to be perfect. After you have collected your images, it is best to set a time limit and just sit down and do it. You can always start another one later. Keep in mind that you are not trying to create a lasting work of art. The benefits are in the process as much as in the finished product.

If you feel you need motivation or inspiration, consider creating a collage workshop of your own. All you need is a few friends, materials, and good music. The value of this exercise increases tremendously when done in a group. You can swap magazines, and get ideas from looking at each other's work. When the collages are complete (usually two to three hours later) you can take turns sharing how you feel about the finished product. Group members can also offer feedback about what they see, and even suggest stores where the desired clothing might be found. If you are worried that your statement might be vague and unclear, when you see it in comparison to others, you will see just how distinctive it really is.

I think the best reason for working in a group was articulated by Emily, a participant in a recent workshop. "In a vacuum, being different feels uncomfortable, but in a group it feels good." Our uniqueness needs to be acknowledged before it can be appreciated. Looking at your collage and seeing a reflection of yourself that you like is a joyful and exhilarating experience.

It is fascinating to watch your dynamic spirit evolve. I have done a collage every season for four years, and I am astonished by the changes. When I look at my collages I am struck by how clearly what we want to see on the outside mirrors the corresponding development inside. I can remember how what was happening in my life at the time influenced my self-image and self-concept. Looking back over my collages, I see that many of the clothes pictured are now actually hanging in my closet. It did not happen immediately, often taking up to a year before an outfit found its way into my wardrobe. Creating a collage encourages you to stretch, giving the first hint of the vision you would like to create for the future.

11

Successful Shopping

When you Clothe Your Spirit, shopping success is not simply buying something you need at a good price. Success is finding something that makes your heart pound and your knees go weak. It is finding that special something that makes you want to whoop for joy, shouting your delight to passersby. Perhaps I exaggerate slightly for effect, but there is nothing bland or nonchalant about how you feel upon finding the perfect new addition to your wardrobe. You already have clothes. Your goal now is to buy only things that you are in love with.

Shopping for clothes is your chance to put what you have learned about Clothing Your Spirit into practice. If you approach it as an opportunity to express your essence and your beauty, shopping will become an exciting adventure. Imagine holding up a garment and asking yourself, "Is this fresh and charming?" or "Is this dramatic and streamlined?" (Substitute your choices.) Reflecting upon the ability of an outfit to express your spirit is far more entertaining than simply wondering if it fits. When you consider shopping as the pathway to Clothing

Your Spirit, your approach changes. This does not guarantee that it will be easy, because shopping can be hard work. But the experience will be such an improvement that any negative feelings you have had about shopping will ultimately be transformed. A rewarding endeavor leads to feeling positive, and positive feelings lead to satisfying results. If you approach a clothing store with gritted teeth expecting the worst, your chances of finding something you love are limited. Start out with an open heart and a light step, and the day promises to be full of rewards.

In spite of my chosen profession, shopping has not always been a great passion of mine. I appreciate the results, the beautiful new clothes, the excitement of seeing myself flattered in a different way, the ease that comes from a closet full of lovely things that fulfill my exact needs. It would be fine with me if the clothes would just materialize and find their way into my life without the searching, the decision making, and the time-consuming effort. I suspect there are a great many people who do not anticipate shopping with relish, and I certainly used to fall into that category. Yet I have learned how to shop successfully, for myself and others, and I have discovered how to minimize the pain and frustration and maximize the rewards.

This chapter will show you how to make shopping work for you. If you have always enjoyed shopping, you are lucky. Now you will have a chance to improve your ability from a talent to an art. The tips I offer will not cover how to recognize the finished seams of quality garments or how to work the sales in search of a good purchase. Information of that type would not help you overcome the feeling of inadequacy that can make you dread the dressing rooms, nor would it prevent you from overspending and filling your closet with too many clothes. What you need to know in order to make your shopping forays successful is how to apply several of the basic ideas of Clothe Your Spirit, including know yourself, trust your instincts, and protect yourself from experiences that damage your self-esteem and sabotage your efforts.

PREPARATION

One of the keys to successful shopping is preparation. The worst damage is usually done during a fit of depression or desperation. The accomplishment of any goal requires intelligent planning. By reading this far, you have already taken a number of steps that will make your next shopping trip a more rewarding one. The previous chapters explore a great many areas, and it would be impossible to retain every discovery you made. However, you do need access to that valuable information. The trick is to summarize the insights you have gained into no more than ten words, and then carry them with you like a refrain.

Keep in mind your spirit, your assets, and your present clothing needs, and look at everything with an eye for whether it meets your criteria. For example, when I am shopping for myself I keep in mind my spirit (straightforward, sophisticated, sensuous, sparkling), my assets (breasts, midriff, hips, legs), and whatever clothing needs I am concentrating on at the time. When I shop for my clients I do exactly the same thing. On a 5" × 7" note card I put small swatches of their best colors and the ten key words that summarize what I am looking for. Holly's card says, "fun, fresh, little-kid; tall, long legs, delicate upper body; layered work clothes, casual weekend wear." Debbie's card says, "streamlined, dramatic, delightful; tall, straight lines, broad shoulders; festive evening and party clothes."

The "ten key words" technique makes it easier to focus and to make good choices. It helps you make rejections more easily and quickly, and if you let your refrain play loudly enough, it can also drown out any strains of the tune "fat, hopeless, and awkward" some of you may be used to hearing.

The advantage of using key words is that they suggest an idea rather than demand that you conform to a rigid list. Finding clothes you love requires being open to what is available. You cannot shop for wonderful things using a list like the one you take to the market. The perfect blue blouse is not waiting for you on aisle three. If you are looking for a specific item, there is a good chance you will find one; whether you will absolutely love the outfit you create with it is another question. A list can help you clarify your needs by providing examples, but if you diligently stick to it, you may overlook something extraordinary hanging just beside it.

Your attitude should be like that of an athlete—loose but ready. Think of Clothing Your Spirit as an adventure full of surprises. Try looking at shopping in much the same way as you would approach taking a journey, perhaps a vacation by car. For example, you are going to drive from California to New York, and you plan to take one month to do it. You carefully study your maps and work out an itinerary. Everything goes according to plan until day five, when it rains too much to comfortably continue. Luxuriating in the unexpected respite, you spend two days holed up in your hotel room, reading novels and ordering room service. During the second week you make some new friends, and they invite you to spend the weekend on their desert ranch. Your plans change, you readjust, and you still make it to New York on time. When you put together your wardrobe you know basically where you want to end up, but sticking too closely to a specific plan might cause you to miss the main objective—to find clothes that you love.

The next step in the process of getting ready for shopping is to know your resources. Browsing with the intention of getting ideas is a great way to learn about what is available in your area. If you usually gravitate to the same few stores, spend some time researching alternatives. Since the large department stores can be overwhelming, it is helpful to break them down into sections. Concentrate on discovering the departments you feel comfortable in instead of attempting to take on the entire store. If you usually stick to the department stores, branch out by discovering some of the smaller shops and speciality stores. The merchandise in a boutique reflects the preferences of the buyer or owner; you might find one whose taste is in alignment with yours. New discount stores and outlets spring up all the time. If you are interested in bargain hunting, investigate some of the options. Many large cities have resource books that do the legwork for you.

While most of us are interested in saving money, don't automatically assume that an off-price store is the best way to do it. You are not doing yourself any favors if you buy something because you are in love with the price tag rather than the garment. If you think you "should" shop in a discount store but find you never feel satisfied with your purchases, branch out. If you feel the special attention available in a smaller shop would help you, don't force yourself to shop in a large store, discount or otherwise. Your objective is to find things that you love, so shop wherever you can best accomplish your goal.

While you are researching your clothing-store options, window shop for ideas. It is a great way to find out what fashions are available. Walk through your local shopping area and see if any of the stores have merchandise similar to what you put on the collage you created in the previous chapter. Most stores display the next season's clothing far in advance of when you actually need them, so take your time and look for ideas and inspiration. Spending some time browsing gives you a chance to further consider your needs and clarify what appeals to you without the emotional roller coaster of trying things on and making decisions.

There is no need to always prepare as thoroughly as I have described each time you want to go shopping. Buying clothes is time consuming enough without additional days devoted to research. But planning requires thoughtful consideration, and even a small amount of preparation will help you avoid the pitfalls of desperation buying. I hear over and over again the disappointment and dissatisfaction that comes from frantically dashing in some-

Now I don't go shopping until I am sure what it is I really want. I don't go in and decide to buy something just because I am in the store—I go with a purpose in mind, which narrows down what I am looking for. If I see something wonderful I might try it on, but I won't buy it unless it fits both my spirit and my lifestyle.

Debbie

I usually gain 5-10 pounds in the winter and lose it in the spring. I don't get frantic, in fact I hardly get concerned. If I am a little heavier, I buy bigger clothes. I just make sure they are fashionable, in good colors, and things that I love.

Serita

where and buying something, whether to fill a wardrobe need or an emotional emptiness. There is nothing wrong with impulse buying if it is done in the spirit of fun, and backed up by an awareness of yourself and your needs. Discovering the perfect item and spontaneously purchasing it is exhilarating and rewarding.

Your attitude when you walk into the store will very likely determine the outcome. However, I am not telling you that you always have to feel good and like yourself before you go shopping. If you arc feeling lousy and desperately need clothes, rouse your energy, set a date, and go do it. Setting a "when-I-lose-ten-pounds-date" does not count. When people set a shopping date with me they are committed, and if they are unable to reach a weight loss goal in the interim, I politely tell them, "We're going anyway!" Despite the reluctance they feel, they are always delightfully surprised at how much better things look than they expected. The positive frame of mind that comes from knowing you can look wonderful exactly the way you are will stimulate you to look even better, and help you to lose weight if that is your objective. Commit yourself to going shopping, and go with your head held high. Keep in mind you are going to Clothe Your Spirit and create an expression of the fine human being that you are. If you find you still feel reluctant, make a point of taking short excursions. A trip does not have to be long to be effective.

If you are going to go with someone, the two of you can make a pact and set a date. If the winter months are hard on your self-esteem, it is especially worthwhile to do this in early spring. If the approach of bathing-suit season starts you panicking in February, reassure yourself with the promise of a satisfying shopping day in April.

SHOPPING WITH A PARTNER

Carefully pick and choose who you take shopping with you. You may feel the need to take someone along to help you, but often what they offer isn't help at all. Making a poor choice about who to take with you is much worse than going alone. It is too easy to ignore your own voice in favor of another's opinion. The ideal person may or may not be your mother, your husband, or your best friend. What follows is an outline of the qualities of an ideal shopping companion. See if any of the people in your life fit the bill.

The most important quality you should look for in a shopping partner is an unshakeable belief that you are beautiful and absolutely perfect the way you are. When someone feels that way about you, he or she will help you find clothes that enhance your beauty, not merely camouflage your flaws. That person expects you to look great, and when you don't, she sees that it is the garment, not you. Being hard to please is her greatest asset. If someone thinks you should lose a few pounds, your complexion is too ruddy, or your tastes are too ethnic, she will not hold out for something perfect. She can not help but encourage you to settle for so-so.

The next most important characteristic your partner should have is a heartfelt desire for you to succeed. Partners want you to find the perfect thing, they don't want you to settle, and they truly want you to be happy. They want to understand what you are trying to do, and they want to help.

The perfect person to take shopping wants to go with you and does not have to be coerced. She has plenty of time, and won't rush you while you make a decision, or worse yet, convince you something is "good enough" so the day can come to an end. Not everyone has the necessary endurance for shopping, and unless you plan to make it a short trip, you would be well advised not to depend on an impatient person's opinion.

Although it is not as important as the above qualities, a certain amount of fashion finesse is important. Go with someone whose taste you admire. The two of you do not have to look alike or share a fondness for the same type of clothing, but your partner should have a good eye for line and style.

The attributes of a person who does not support you can be quite subtle. It may be a person whom you otherwise love and depend upon, but when it comes to clothes selection, that person is not able to give you the assistance you need. Several shopping partnerships do not work as well as you might expect. Mothers and daughters are a natural combination, but because of their relationship, it is difficult for them to consider each other objectively. "What good old Mom really needs," the daughter may decide, "is to quit looking so 'over-the-hill' and start looking more 'hip' (like me)." Mom, if she happens to feel slightly frumpy and out of date, agrees. What the daughter may not be able to see is that her mother has reached a time in her life that is both beautiful and expressive in an entirely new way. A mother often has the same problem of not recognizing her daughter as the individual she has become. The fact that her daughter wants to look a certain way, especially if it is exactly like all of her friends, can be frustrating to a mother longing for her own self-expression. Every spirit evolves at its own rate, and each of us can only choose what we feel comfortable with at the time.

It is difficult for any of us to leave our familiar roles behind, and mothers and daughters often repeat patterns that are not very helpful. One of my regular clients, who is familiar with the Clothe Your Spirit concept, asked me to help her daughter do some last-minute shopping in hopes of finding a dress she could wear to a wedding the following day. We only needed one outfit, and as far as I was concerned we had all the time in the world to find the daughter something she loved. But as the afternoon progressed, I was surprised to see my client and friend transform into a typically impatient mother. Instead of allowing her daughter the opportunity to decide if she liked an outfit, she would try to settle the issue by saying abruptly, "Well, is it better than anything else you have to wear tomorrow?" This mother could not help the fact that she had waited too many times for a daughter to finish a task, and years of impatience had built up. I do not want to deprive mothers and daughters of any shared future shopping pleasure, but it is helpful to be aware of the roles that are so easy to unconsciously fall into.

A good friend is one of our favorite choices for a shopping mate, but take care to choose cautiously. Even if you enjoy a friend's company, you may suspect she is just envious enough of you to subtly sabotage your intentions. If someone is insecure about her own beauty, it can be hard to wholeheartedly encourage someone else's. It is appropriate to feel compassion for this individual, but don't let her limitations become yours. The opposite can also be true. If your friend is totally wrapped up in her own wonderfulness, she may be unable to take your needs seriously. Even if she has fabulous taste and is always exquisitely turned out, she will not be of any real help to you unless she cares as much about your success as she does her own.

Now that I have gone after your mother and your best friend, you may (correctly) suspect that I am going to pick on the man in your life. We feel the need to include our "significant other" in our decisions because his opinion matters so much to us. Taking him along does not ensure that you will find the clothes that look as good as you both are hoping for. Husbands and boyfriends often have an idea or an image of what they want to see, but they may have no real idea of how to accomplish it. This can lead to a frustrating day for everyone concerned. When I take a woman shopping, there is always some initial concern over what the important person in her life will think of a new style of clothing. As the day goes on, the uncertainty is replaced by a growing eagerness to return home and share the excitement. When you feel confident about something being right for you, others in your life cannot help but recognize it. When I ask my clients about the response to their new clothes, they often tell me that their men say, "That is exactly how I wanted you to look; I just didn't know how to tell you to do it."

You should have a good idea of who are the best

people in your life to take shopping. In my case, one of my favorites happens to be my father. He expects me to look great, and waits to give his approval until his vision of me is confirmed. We live in different cities and do not often have the opportunity to see each other, but shopping with him taught me what supportive assistance could be like. My husband, on the other hand, has great taste and valuable suggestions, but the tortured look on his face after more than fifteen minutes makes him a less than ideal companion. Before your next shopping trip, ask yourself who you really feel good about shopping with, and seek that person out. It is not necessary to shun everyone else, but be realistic about the difficulty of avoiding the influence of another's opinion.

If you communicate your needs clearly, you can tell your companion exactly how to best assist you. I have often wished I knew cloning techniques so I could give myself the same assistance I am able to give my clients. Then I discovered just how wonderful a supportive friend could be. Several years ago one of my clients and I became fast friends, so we dispensed with our professional relationship and began shopping together for fun. As our friendship developed, she was able to glimpse my spirit as well as recognize the vulnerabilities and insecurities I felt about my body. At first she was anxious about advising me, but I told her all she had to do was imagine she was meeting me for the first time and decide if the image she saw was making the correct impression.

We approached our first shopping trip together fairly formally, putting the date on our calendars and taking a day off work. We thought through our goals in advance and discussed them over breakfast. My friend told me her biggest weakness was not being discriminating enough. An easy fit, she had trouble turning down anything, and had the overstuffed closet to prove it. She needed me to help her wait for the truly special garments. I told her my problem was a tendency to choose things that were overly baggy. I was ready for garments that were more body-conscious, but I was also anxious about revealing too much. I wanted the opinion of someone I could trust.

Not only was our shopping day successful, it was great fun. We stuck together when salespeople tried to tell us how wonderful it *all* looked. If fatigue threated to overcome either of us, we took a break. When things looked awful, we laughed and made faces, and when they looked great we cheered each other on. By talking things over, we were able to stay within the constraints of our budgets, the realities of our lifestyles, and still choose only things we loved. My friend found a stunning sweater with a price tag to match, and decided to pass after realizing that she would only wear it once a year, tops. I had to make a choice about a jacket (which was something I desperately needed) at such a great price I could hardly bear to turn it down, but I decided against it after facing the fact that it stopped just short of looking wonderful. By focusing on the things we were gaining, we were able to walk away from the other items without feeling deprived. We returned home that night, exhausted but exultant.

Our shopping day together was a real revelation for me. I had shopped with friends since I was a pre-teenager, but I had never experienced a day like this, so completely fulfilling and successful. You can create the same kind of day with one of your friends. Talk about the Clothe Your Spirit concept. Spend an afternoon together, looking at magazines or making a collage. Discuss your goals, set a shopping date, and then stick by each other. Learn how you can help your companion, and tell your companion how she or he can help you. Don't wait until you are frantic about needing something to wear and drag along whoever is willing. I can guarantee that you won't be as pleased with the results.

If there is no one in your life right now that you feel comfortable asking, and you dread going alone, there are still alternatives. A professional image consultant provides expertise and undivided attention.

Be sure to choose a professional even more carefully than you would choose a friend. A professional title is no guarantee that he or she will possess the important qualities I have discussed. If the cost of an image consultant is prohibitive, check into the complimentary shopping services available at the major department stores. The upcoming chapter, "Finding Help," offers detailed advice about choosing professional assistance.

MAKING DECISIONS

Although it is important to carefully consider your shopping partner, sometimes the best person to take is no one at all. Going alone is not necessarily an undesirable substitute for shopping with a companion. Shopping solo has some definite advantages and is a skill worth acquiring. For one, your favorite partner may not be available. Two, the pace a partner sets may not always be in tune with yours. Three, and most importantly, you need to be able to trust your own feelings about whether or not a garment is right for you. Shopping alone gives you a chance to tune into your inner voice until you are able to hear it loudly and clearly. Learning to decipher the tangle of emotions you feel when gazing into a mirror takes a little practice, but once you learn to count on your own instincts, they will never let you down.

When an outfit is right for you, the feeling is quite distinct. You look in the mirror, and your instant reaction is "Perfect!" A little bubble of excitement wells up inside of you, and a feeling of satisfaction and happiness spreads through your body. You begin to envision yourself wearing the outfit to a specific occasion or around a certain person. You preen a little in front of the mirror, maybe even strut about in search of admiring comments. Then you take if off, purchase it, and leave the store, delighted to have found the ideal thing.

Knowing how you feel about a garment is not always so clear cut. Most of us are more familiar with the tense moments of anxiety when it comes time

It is easy for me now to know when something is ME. I can tell by looking at something whether it is going to work or not before I even try it on.

Holly

to make a decision. The next time you find yourself having dificulty making a choice, consider some of the factors that might be causing your uncertainty. Are there a lot of people hovering around telling you it looks terrific? Even though you have your doubts, do you wonder if they might be right? It is possible for something to look great "on" you and still not be right "for" you. Maybe you know something about your spirit that they don't. It is entirely possible that you might not be ready for the outfit in question. No matter how fantastic something looks, only you can know if you will feel comfortable wearing it. Other conflicting emotions may be at the root of your indecision. Deep inside you may be aware that the garment is not something you need, but you are anticipating the pain you will feel if you cannot own it. Or, you might be aware that it is not great and are allowing your opinion to be swayed because it is something you are in particular need of. It is no fun to go home empty-handed! It is also possible that none of the above is true, that the outfit is perfectly wonderful and you are not used to the "newness" or boldness of it.

What should you do in this situation? The first thing to do is to walk around the store. Casually glance in the mirrors as you pass by. Try to relax, take your time, and keep walking and glancing until a clear reaction begins to develop. If you still feel torn, take it off, put it on hold, and leave the store. Go off by yourself somewhere quiet, and see if you feel relieved or sad. Ask yourself what is triggering your uncertainty. Do not let anyone force you into a decision by telling you the garments are "going like hot-cakes" and that the last one in your size will certainly be gone by the time you get back. If they won't hold it for you, leave anyway. I have personally used the "flee" technique at least fifty times, and only once was a blouse I decided I wanted not available when I came back for it. Missing out that one time was worth all the other times I avoided filling my closet with clothes I was not in love with or didn't need. My dilemmas usually stem from uncertainty about the cost or the garment's overall usefulness, and I have always been glad I took the time to make a well-thought-out decision.

Tuning into your emotions and feelings about an outfit is the best way to make a decision, but there are also several guidelines worth remembering. First of all, there is no such thing as a garment that "almost" fits. Either it fits or it doesn't. No amount of disappointment or wishing it weren't so will change the fact that an imperfect fit will stay an imperfect fit. During the excitement of the moment you might convince yourself that the small droop in the shoulders or the "tiny" tug on the button will not bother you, but once you begin wearing it you will find yourself with a garment you cannot fully enjoy. The second part of this rule follows the same theme: Never buy anything that cannot be worn immediately unless you have a specific plan for alterations. If you buy something hoping it will fit when you lose a few pounds, you will discover by the time you lose the necessary weight and ease the tightness that another area of the garment will no longer fit correctly.

The last rule is really the theme of this chapter, but it bears repeating. Only buy clothes you are in love with. It is easy enough to enjoy a garment when it is new, but the novelty fades rapidly. If you merely like a garment when you purchase it, the transition to dislike will happen too quickly. Recall what being in love with a garment should feel like, and ask yourself if you honestly feel that way. Can you hardly wait to wear it? Do you love it enough to buy all the necessary accessories? If the answers are yes, and it fits the needs of your lifestyle, then buy it with a light heart, knowing you will enjoy it for a long time to come.

Salespeople can play a large part in influencing what you finally buy. They can offer everything from valuable assistance to terrible advice. Not all salespeople are biased or acting in their own self-interest; most are trying to help you find something you will be happy with. No matter how sincere their inten-

When I go shopping now, I don't feel like I have to come home with something. If something is wonderful, that's great, and, if not, that's okay. Even if something is wonderful, but it is not the right time for me to buy it, I can still walk out of the store without it; there's not that compulsion anymore.

Debbie

tions, however, their objectivity has to be in question. Several factors can cloud their objectivity, including their commission or sales goals and the sheer number of people they look at every day. "Good" may be good enough for them, but "great" is the only thing good enough for you.

Another limitation is that most salespeople do not know you, therefore they have little awareness of the connection between you as a person and the clothes you are wearing. Now that you know about Clothing Your Spirit, you can make sure your garment goes beyond flattering and expresses the essence of who you are.

Despite any limitations salespeople might have, they can be your best allies. I know I could not manage without them. I treasure their cleverness, their knowledge, and their efficiency. They understand their merchandise and are familiar with how a garment fits. They are usually better at tying a belt or scarf than I am. Cultivate the salespeople you like and trust, and make a point of seeking them out. Explain to them what you need, and let them help you accomplish your goals. But remember that the final decision is up to you, and take care not to depend too much on their opinions. If a salesperson ever pressures you or makes you feel like a country bumpkin, then don't bother to patronize the store again. There are always plenty of fine places to shop. A good salesperson knows honesty will result in satisfied customers, and satisfied customers mean repeat business.

Knowing when to buy (or not to buy!) a garment will become more automatic and comfortable over time. The guidelines stressed here might seem like a great deal to remember at first, but with practice, they will become second nature. Focused concentration improves anything you ever attempt. Once you begin shopping and making decisions, stay with it as long as possible. If you can manage it financially, do the majority of your seasonal purchasing at one time. You will capitalize on your focused attention, and you will be able to find all the necessary pieces

I won't let a salesperson talk me into something because it's the latest thing. It has to be something I feel comfortable in, and I have more confidence now to make that decision myself.

Gloria

to complete your ensembles. Finishing the job will make your life indescribably easier. You will have the clothes you need, and you will be free from the worry and hassle of constantly having to concern yourself with what to wear.

Despite the numerous advantages, I have noticed that most women have a much more difficult time setting aside a sum of money for seasonal shopping than men do. Even though it is not nearly as effective, women seem to feel more comfortable shopping in bits and pieces. It may feel as if you are spending less, but in reality, you are probably just staying unconscious about the overall amount. Face the fact that you are going to need clothes, which means spending money, and be up front about it, especially with yourself. Clothing Your Spirit is an important, not a clandestine, activity. If you share finances with a partner, talk about your needs as openly as possible. To make a change (and Clothing Your Spirit can be a big change) you need support. For many women, being open about their desires takes a great deal of courage. If you sincerely try to do what is right for you, you will find approval from those who love you.

Do not sabotage all that can be gained from Clothing Your Spirit by spending more money than you can afford. The guilt you feel will undo all the positive aspects. When you are doing your pre-shopping research, look for stores that stay within your price range. If you are just browsing and have no intention of buying, it is fine to look at the most expensive merchandise. But when you are ready to make some purchases, do not begin by trying on clothing you cannot afford. This can only depress you and make everything else look shabby by comparison. Don't set yourself up to go home feeling deprived. Whatever your budget is, you can look great. The intelligent way you approach shopping is more important than the amount of money you have to spend.

Make sure you know the return policy before leaving the store. If it is hard for you to feel certain about your decisions, concentrate your shopping on stores

I spent twice the money on clothes two years ago that I do now. It didn't seem like it, because I'd buy one thing here and one thing there. Now I buy what I am going to buy and that's the end of it.

Debbie

that are liberal about returns and exchanges. There may still be times when you find yourself shopping simply because you are in a lousy mood and you think something new will cheer you up. If you are determined to buy something, go ahead—and don't feel guilty about it. When your mood passes, try on everything you purchased and ask yourself if you really love it. If you find you did make a mistake (and we all do), don't fret over it; just take it back.

There is one way to make searching for the ideal garment work against you, and if you already tend to be a perfectionist, it is a pitfall you should be careful to avoid. Do not make your expectations so unrealistic that you will never find anything. The clothes are not going to leap off the racks at you. Sometimes it is necessary to consider a garment more than once. Be realistic, stay flexible and open, don't expect miracles, and remember that shopping can be hard work. Fun but, at times, hard work.

Even with the best intentions of following the instructions for successful shopping, it is still possible to have an occasional terrible experience. You know the kind of day I mean—every dressing room is filled with zombies lying in wait to reflect an ugly, unpleasing view of your flaws in a seemingly endless series of mirrors. Nothing fits, everything looks awful, the merchandise in the stores is depressing, and the one thing you like costs ten times more than you can afford. Your feet hurt, your shoulders ache, and everyone seems to be happily toting bulging shopping bags except you. The fact that you feel like slinking away in search of food makes it even worse, because you are convinced that too much eating is the cause of your present problems.

When a day like this occurs, give in to your need to comfort yourself by getting away from the frenzy of shoppers and find a quiet and comfortable corner. Order a soothing cup of tea or hot chocolate and start to relax, letting go of the tension and frustration. When you begin to feel calmer, put the experience into perspective. Do not allow yourself to be devastated by one bad experience. You are still a beautiful and valuable person, both inside and out. Consider why the day turned out badly. Have you had bad luck at these same stores before? Were you unprepared emotionally? Ask yourself if you were shopping for the wrong reasons. Your shopping will not be successful if you are generally disgusted or needy in a way that clothes will not fulfill. Did you go against your better judgment and take someone shopping that you knew would not be supportive? It is possible that you were prepared in every way, but the clothing you were looking at was just not right for you. It often seems that designers create clothing with no awareness of what a woman's body looks like. Sometimes I have to search hard for my clothes, but I refuse to be daunted by unsuccessful experiences. I know I will eventually find the perfect thing, both for myself and for my clients. When clothing does not look good on you, don't take it personally. Successful shopping takes time and practice, and if you don't allow yourself to become discouraged, you will ultimately be richly rewarded.

An unsuccessful day will be the exception rather than the rule. When you take a positive approach to shopping by concentrating on Clothing Your Spirit, you will accomplish exactly what you set out to do. My shopping service regularly works itself out of a job, because after a trip or two my clients grow confident and often go off on their own. The new insights they have about themselves help them to clarify their needs, but the real reason behind their independence is that, for the first time, they feel great about their ability to look wonderful in clothes. Their experience with me has been a successful one, and nothing succeeds like success.

Learn how to make shopping work for you. Whatever doubts you may have about your appearance, head for the stores knowing you are ready—prepared, positive, flexible, and open. Take a friend along, and enjoy the deepening of your relationship when you share a new approach to shopping together. When the clothes don't work, blame the dressing room zombie instead of your body. Take pride in the fact that you are able to trust yourself to make good decisions. Find out what *you* need to make your shopping day a successful one. You can turn shopping into an activity you feel good about, and when you do, there will be nothing keeping you from Clothing Your Spirit. The clothes available in the stores right now are the only tools you need to express your essence more fully.

12

Express Yourself With Accessories

There is no need to let the mention of the word "accessories" send a chill of fear down your spine. Accessorizing your clothing does not require a special talent or knack that you were born without. Being skilled at adding the final touches to your clothes is not the difference between the well dressed (them) and the unfinished (you). To look your best you need to complete your outfit, but there is nothing complicated or mysterious about it. To appropriately accessorize you clothes, it is not necessary to follow the latest trends. What you do need to know is what accessories are for and how to successfully use them.

There are two types of accessories: the kind that finish an outfit and the ones that add an extra something to it. Some accessories do both. The most important role accessories play in the development of your wardrobe is the way they pull the completed look together. Whenever you buy a new outfit, the first thing you should do is stand in front of the mirror and ask yourself, "What is missing?" Working from the ground up, begin with your feet. Do you

A man I was dating for awhile told me the first thing he noticed about me was my great pink shoes. He didn't notice my face or anything I had on. He was looking down when I walked in for an interview, and he remembered this charming young lady with pink shoes.

Holly

own shoes in the appropriate color, heel height, and style? If not, you will have to plan on getting a pair. Will you need to purchase a specific color of hosiery to tie your hemline and shoe together? Does your new garment have beltloops, or does the waistline need to be cinched in? If so, a belt is in order. Do you have one that will work or will you need to find a new belt? Does the neckline look unfinished, perhaps in need of a scarf or necklace? Do the little holes in your ears necessitate coordinating earrings? Finally, you need a handbag whose color and size compliments your outfit. (Tip: If you need to find new accessories, start by asking the salesperson to suggest possibilities from the store you are in.)

It is only necessary to add an accessory when a portion of your outfit looks unfinished. A good, hard look in the mirror will tell you what areas require your attention. The information you need to appropriately accessorize your clothes is available to you simply by looking. What is needed is a willingness to follow through and find what is missing.

The reason so much attention is placed on accessories is because they offer you the option to do more. Used appropriately, they can go beyond "finishing" an outfit by adding to it. Don't pressure yourself into thinking you must do that in order to look great; it is just not true. If you have bought a wonderful outfit in a color that flatters you and expresses your spirit, and you have added the appropriate shoes and jewelry, you will already look fantastic. Anything beyond that is simply an opportunity for you to have a little fun.

When you are shopping, watch for the things that catch your eye and immediately appeal to you. You might be drawn to a small, veiled hat or a pair of jade-green leather gloves, an art-deco pin or a playful straw bag. Now that you know something of your spirit in terms of fashion, you can recognize why an item commands your attention. If you find an accessory you fall in love with, you can buy it knowing that at some point you will be able to incorporate it into your wardrobe.

The accessories that both complete an outfit and express your spirit are always a treat to find. You will get a real lift when you discover something that not only fulfills the intended function but is interesting and expressive as well. If you love the seashore, this might be a belt with an unusual shell buckle or an earring shaped like a scallop. As you get used to approaching shopping with an awareness of both yourself and your needs, you will stumble across more and more of these "finds."

Looking for accessories requires the same attitude and plan for action as any other type of shopping. Your first step is to evaluate your needs. List your clothes and the items necessary to complete your outfit. At this point, a written itemization is helpful, as long as you remember to keep it flexible. For example, list "shoes for blue dress" and "shoes for white dress" rather than "blue shoes" and "white shoes." If you keep an open mind, you might discover a third color that would work well for both outfits.

When you consider purchasing an accessory, make certain that it both fits your lifestyle and fulfills the need you are buying it for. It is easy to get swept off your feet by a gorgeous shoe or handbag, but if it spoils the comfort and practicality of the outfit you are buying it for, it doesn't matter how beautiful it is. The same is true of buying something because you are attracted to the great price. If the shoe pinches or an inexpensive belt slips out of the buckle, it is no bargain. If an item does not function as it is intended, you will ultimately have to replace it with one that works better. Shopping for accessories requires patience, because what you are looking for can be difficult to find. It is easy to convince yourself that a less than perfect belt will "do" if you are dying to wear your new jumpsuit, but if you persevere, your outfit will look that extra measure better. If you let your impatience get the better of you, you will probably never feel fully satisfied.

Unfortunately, buying "finishing" accessories is not a place where you can effectively cut corners.

I saw a gorgeous pair of shoes. They were blue-grey leather with rose-colored pleated fans on them. I had to have them. For these shoes I would buy an outfit to go with them. They are yummy.

Serita

It is really helpful for me to make a list so I know what I am looking for.

Holly

145

It is better to buy fewer outfits and concentrate on finishing the ones you have. This does not mean you necessarily have to spend a great deal of money. Quality is always important, but you need to concentrate on buying what you can comfortably afford that best does the job. Consider the cost of an accessory in the same way you would any clothing purchase, remembering that it has to function as well as look good.

The first rule of shopping applies to accessories as well: Always try to buy something you love. Obviously, you won't feel wild excitement when you buy a simple belt, but you should be pleased. Don't force yourself to buy anything you feel is functional but boring. A few summers ago I was looking for white sandals. While trying on a suitable pair my eyes strayed to the same style in hot pink. I knew immediately which pair I felt excited about. I decided to leave the white ones and take the pink ones, and, although I was unsure what I would wear them with, by the end of last summer they were so worn I regretfully had to throw them away. A basic color might be a necessary backdrop to an outfit, but don't be afraid to experiment if a neutral color leaves you cold.

The accessories you buy are another tool available for the outward expression of your spirit. Add a color to your wardrobe and watch it lift your spirits. If the blooming daffodils heralding the approach of spring bring on a longing for something yellow, join the celebration by accessorizing a neutral outfit with a yellow purse, belt, and earrings. Adding polish to your clothes is not so much a skill as it is an awareness of your spirit and a tuning in to what you feel compelled to convey. The expression of your spirit can be enhanced by the accessories you select. The finishing touches shown on the women in this book are simple, but each is unique to the individual. Sunny, glowing Gloria adds a nosegay of flowers to her lapel. Serita chooses a traditional foulard scarf to add a soft but classic touch to her white dress. Holly loves accessorizing her clothes with fun, colorful necklaces, bracelets, and earrings, but Debbie prefers to keep her choices streamlined and simple. A red and white polka-dot scarf is perfect for Holly, a strand of ivory beads an ideal expression for Debbie. There are no fashion "rules," only options that allow you to select what is right for you.

When you are shopping for accessories, keep in mind that "appropriate" is the key word. Appropriate for your lifestyle, your budget, your spirit, and finally the overall look of the outfit itself. It is better to keep it simple than to overdo it. Not every outfit is enhanced by the addition of extra items, especially if they detract from your assets. When it comes to accessories, you should buy only what you need, love, and feel comfortable with. Give accessories the attention they deserve, and they will create complete, polished outfits you will love to wear. At that point, the well dressed (them) will become the finished . . . YOU.

My accessories stay really simple. The less I have in accessories, the better I feel. Whatever it is has to make the same statement the outfit does.

Debbie

When I am looking for accessories, most of the time I look for something that stands out. But not always, because I buy dainty little earrings and delicate gold chains to express my feminine side.

Holly

13

Finding Help: Choosing the Image Consultant Who Is Right For You

Enlisting the aid of a professional to help you Clothe Your Spirit can be a tremendous boost. An image consultant will guide you through the areas you feel uncertain about and open up new avenues of awareness. The frustrating experience of dealing with your own wardrobe can be replaced by satisfying results. A wise image consultant can help you learn to fully express your beauty. The effectiveness of the time you spend together depends on whom you choose. In a field filled with as many approaches as there are image consultants, you need to find the individual who is right for you. I cannot offer you a totally unbiased overview, but I can tell you what you can expect from the services of an image professional and how to go about finding one you will be happy with.

If you have ever shopped around for a new physician or therapist, you probably spent some time looking closely at their beliefs and methods. Whom you select to entrust your self-image to should be chosen as carefully as any professional service that aids an aspect of your well-being. Referrals are the logical place to begin, because satisfied customers are usually delighted to share their good fortune with others. People do not necessarily want to announce the reason behind their radiant new look, but compliments and sincere interest will often prompt the individual to be forthcoming. If you do not know anyone who can refer you, talk to people you know and trust in a related field. I work in conjunction with career counselors, job recruiters, health-care centers, fitness clubs, and women's groups. The yellow pages often have listings, but many professionals prefer to take only referrals, so be sure to ask around.

No matter how glowing the reference, you should meet the person and form your own opinion. Before you begin making calls or appointments, clarify for yourself what type of help you feel you need. Would you like information on color or make-up? Do you lack the time, talent, or inclination for clothes shopping? Are you generally dissatisfied with the way you look and think you could do better? Are you curious about exploring the relationship between your outer expression and your inner self? The response you receive when you voice your concerns and express your areas of interest will tell you if you have come to the right place.

When you talk to an image consultant, the first thing you will want to know is what type of services are provided. My service offers everything discussed in this book, from discovering your spirit to selecting the final accessories. My clients can do as much or as little as they desire, but I do progress in a certain order; closet cleaning and lifestyle assessment always precede shopping. I offer various follow-up workshops and classes, which many organizations do as well. Every image consultant works in a way she or he finds effective, whether it is shopping by the hour or arranging to bring completed outfits to your place of business. Additional services are often available, including everything from home decorating to party planning. Some consultants charge by the hour, others by the task. Fees vary, and price is no indication of the quality of the service. If you like someone a great deal but the costs seem prohibitive, see if you can arrange to do a small portion of their service at a time. Don't be shy about asking. Explain how much money you have to work with, and find out what they can do for you.

After you have made your preliminary inquiries, it is time to meet the individual in person. This is the most important part of the selection process. The chemistry between the two of you will determine the quality of your relationship. You should feel an immediate attraction and an excitement about what he or she has to offer you. A little apprehension is normal, but you should not feel uncomfortable or intimidated. From the first meeting you should be aware of the consultant's compassion and sensitivity to you and your needs. You are going to open up and share parts of yourself you might feel protective about, and you need to feel safe and secure before you can honestly proceed.

You should feel confident that the person you are talking to is not going to try to remake you in his or her image. The most important talent an image consultant can possess is an ability to let you discover your own uniqueness. Remember the characteristics of the perfect person to take with you that I outlined in the chapter on shopping? That person, first, thinks you are already perfect and wants to see you enhance your beauty; second, wants to take the time to understand your needs; third, cares that you succeed; and finally, is patient. A good image consultant will possess all of these qualities, and you will intuitively sense whether they do by talking to them.

No matter how great your rapport, the absolute bottom line is appearance. You are choosing an "image" consultant, not a therapist. You should feel no qualifications about the consultant's taste, clothing, make-up, hair, or the image she or he presents to the world. Even though your look will undoubtedly be different, the consultant's style will come through to a certain extent. I recently worked with a man who said, very touchingly, "I want to look just

Choose an image consultant who is interested in you as a person, who wants to clothe you as that total person and bring out your strong points.

Gloria

like you." You should feel the same way. It is easy to let a feeling of kinship or a developing spark of friendship between you and the consultant cloud your objectivity, but stand firm on the importance of the professional's appearance. In order to bring out the best in you, the person you choose for help should have fully personally realized the same; the consultant's own image must be first rate.

The atmosphere of the workplace is a good indication of ability and professionalism. The colors should be pleasing, the lighting adequate but subtle. The environment should be free enough of distractions that you are able to feel completely comfortable and relaxed. The place of business is important to an image professional who takes work seriously.

Visiting the consultant's office or salon is your opportunity to look at any supportive materials. Don't just believe benignly or take the words of glowing testimonials presented to you that the consultant has talent. Ask for specifics. If you are considering having your colors done, the investigation you do at this point is especially important. You can learn a great deal of information from a completed color chart if you know what to look for.

The most important aspect of your color palette is that it is unique to you. Any type of "pre-packaged" method will not give you the specifics you need. A vast range of colors with a multitude of fabric swatches is not necessarily a good indication of an accurate analysis. The finished color chart should be refined and specific, and all the colors should be in harmony with each other. You should be able to purchase an article of clothing that matches any color on your chart with complete confidence that it will coordinate with the other items in your wardrobe. The palette should look balanced and complete with colors that are both neutral and strong. There should be adequate emphasis on texture as well as color. The presentation of the colors should be clear and easy to understand. Don't be impressed by polished packaging, something the industry has down pat. Look for substance, not slickness.

If you want assistance in developing your wardrobe, ask to see photographs or a portfolio. If none is available, ask for references, but remember, "One picture is worth a thousand (glowing) words." When you decide on a wardrobe consultant, make certain he or she is planning to allow enough time to get to know you and your needs. If the shopping service consists of a one-hour time slot, you will not be getting the attention you deserve. You might take home clothes that look good on you, but it is unlikely you will learn anything lasting from it.

Any clothes you purchase will ultimately wear out, but your experience with an image consultant should enrich your life and help you make rewarding choices in the future. If you decide you would benefit from the services a professional has to offer, your most important consideration is what you hope to accomplish. Whatever you desire, it is undoubtedly available. There is no shortage of people or approaches to choose from.

We are just beginning to explore the intricacies of the word "image." Is it "style," as the fashion magazines suggest, or is it the outward expression of an inner uniqueness? Each of us is free to interpret it in her own way, and to ask for help in defining it if necessary. It is a rewarding experience to see one's familiar face and figure reflected in a new light. Talented assistance is available to help you enhance your beauty and allow it to reach its fullest potential.

The first time I had my colors done, there were a million colors and I just used the ones I liked the best. I didn't get anything out of it because there was no follow up about what to do with the colors after you got them.

Debbie

If you are hiring an image consultant, do it once and get educated. Get a return on your investment. It will be worth it.

Serita

It turned my whole life around, and I was conscious of that at the time.

Gloria

14

The Evolving Spirit

I'm still neurotic sometimes. I'm getting ready for summer and I think I should be a size 8 again. But I'm not going to be a size 8, I'm going to be a 10. Yesterday I pulled out my bathing suits, and I put them all on. I knew I was going to be depressed and I said, "It's okay to be depressed and if you don't like how you look in these bathing suits you don't have to keep any of them," so I threw them all away! I decided, okay, those look awful, and I am going to go out and find a bathing suit that doesn't look awful. Or maybe I'll have to decide that what's here (body) and what's up here (head) aren't going to look the same. The next bathing suit I buy will cover up what needs to be covered up, and it will show what needs to be shown. I'm not 16 anymore, I'm 34. My body is never going to look like it did when I was 16; it's the body of a 34-year-old woman, and that's okay.

Debbie

This change in my image definitely affected my move to San Diego. Changing my image made me *more self-confident about what I could do and what I wanted to do. This is my dream spot—I always wanted to live in San Diego. When I got this job offer I thought, "Am I brave enough to do this?" I had gotten the offer once before, and at the time I couldn't do it; but this time I knew I could. Living in California is like vacation land and playland all in one, and that's where I belong. I wanted to be the person I am now, I wanted to play and have fun—those were the things that were important to me. San Diego, this is where I need to be.*

Holly

I am much more satisfied and accepting of my body, more accepting that deterioration is bound to happen. I have good skin, but it is not as firm as it used to be, and it is something I want to accept. When gravity takes over, it is hard to deal with, because society doesn't accept it. I see all the defects, and I have come to the realization there is nothing I can do about them unless I want to spend thousands of dollars on reconstructive surgery, and I am not about to do that. I have other places I want to put my money.

Gloria

The clothes acted as a stimulus for changing other things in my life. I had my hair lightened, and I started using lighter make-up. I have a whole new hairstyle. I had been wearing my hair the same way for approximately sixteen years. It was a complete catharsis, and I became more modern and came into the 1980's. Since I met you, where I live is different, my friends are different, and the composition of my business is different. I think all this is evolutionary. If we meet five years from now and buy different textures, styles, and colors, it is because we are souls evolving. We reflect externally how we feel internally.

Serita

Clothing Your Spirit is not picking a style and sticking to it. Our individual complexities are always searching for a way to vent different moods and desires, and clothing becomes the vehicle that fulfills our yearning for an outward expression of inner transformations. The dynamic aspect of human nature is what makes the process of Clothing Your Spirit so exciting.

How you felt when you started this book is changing as you near its conclusion. Some ideas have sparked immediate responses, and others will serve as catalysts for changing some of the stubborn patterns that are more difficult to resolve. The process of evolution happens gradually, and you will discover that nothing drastic occurs overnight. How you work with the principles of Clothe Your Spirit on a daily basis is what will ultimately make the difference. The decisions you make in a clothing store determine only one aspect of your overall appearance. Each day you have the opportunity to choose how you wish to grow more fully into a realization of your essence.

Getting dressed is something you do every day. When you consider Clothing Your Spirit as a process rather than a goal, putting yourself together each morning takes on added significance. What you select should convey how you feel, enhancing your mood and energy. Each time you look in the mirror, a communication is taking place. When you are assessing what you have on, the message is usually quite clear; either it looks good or it doesn't. Sometimes what looked great last week can mysteriously not feel right today. Learn to expect that favorite outfits will not always look the same each time, and accept it as a natural part of changing and of growing more in tune with your inner awareness. You will avoid being frustrated if you don't try to decide what to wear too far in advance. Give yourself the option to change what you originally had in mind. For example, you have an important meeting coming up and you decide your navy dress would make just the right impression. When the day dawns you find you feel more vulnerable than usual, and your navy dress looks all wrong, like a suit of armour. You glance longingly at your pink angora sweater and skirt, but you are concerned about looking professional. Go ahead and put it on, and see if a different jacket or accessory will help create the professional image you need. If you usually wear it with dressy high heels and drop earrings, switching to a classic pump and pearl studs might make the necessary difference. Even if it means deciding on a third (or fourth) choice, experiment until you look and feel exactly the way you want. If you respond honestly to your need to express how you feel on any given day, the communication you have with others will be enhanced. In order to have the most successful interaction, your inner spirit and its outer manifestation must be in alignment.

When it comes to choosing what to wear, listen to what your subconscious is telling you. It might seem impractical at the time, but trust your intuitive wisdom. During the process of writing this book, I would periodically get the urge to abandon my sweat clothes in favor of one of my nicer outfits. Because I would be sitting at my desk all day, and wearing something special would mean one more trip to the dry cleaners, the notion seemed foolish. But I usually followed my feelings, and looking back now I see how much I needed to see myself looking my best in order to keep my confidence and self-esteem high. The way you look communicates with others, but the message is relayed just as strongly within you. Making the most of your assets is something to be done on a daily basis. If something makes you feel fat, it is especially important to put on something else that doesn't.

When going somewhere special, allow yourself plenty of time both for making changes and for admiring the finished result. It is an age-old stereotype that women spend an inordinate amount of time getting ready. "Primping" can be a positive act, a time for appreciating your beauty. Enjoy the time with yourself. If you consider it a worthwhile

I get dressed according to my mood. If I am feeling a little insecure, I put on something that I know is really wonderful. If I am feeling dramatic, then that is what I wear that day. Or, I might put on something that expresses another part of me. My clothes say all those things.
Debbie

activity, then plan for it. Allow yourself enough time so you can avoid the friction that is caused by making others late.

All of this emphasis on "beauty" and "appearance" might be stirring up some uncomfortable or unresolved feelings. Do you fear that your intelligence or capability might be in question? Do you secretly believe that women who pay too much attention to their looks are vain, shallow, or superficial? Does the message "Don't be conceited!" still ring in your ears? Take a close look at your beliefs about being beautiful. If you feel uneasy about making the most of your assets, you will unconsciously limit yourself.

At the heart of this issue is the question, "Who is your beauty for?" Do you want to look good to please yourself or to impress others? Before you can Clothe Your Spirit, before you can manifest on the outside all that you are inside, you must seek to resolve this question for yourself. We long to express our uniqueness, but we equally crave appreciation and acceptance. It is natural to want to attract those to whom we feel attracted, but we wonder what the best way to go about it is.

One of the rewards of my business is the real-life lessons it allows me to observe. The experiences Janice went through on a recent shopping trip exemply a conflict many of us can relate to. Janice had recently met a man she liked very much, and she called me in a panic because he was taking her to a party the following weekend and she had nothing appropriate to wear. After hearing from a mutual friend that he was looking for an "intellectual Christie Brinkley," she knew how she looked was important to him.

On the Saturday of the party we went looking for a dress. At our first stop Janice found a sleek black dress that showed off her slim, athletic figure to its fullest advantage. Yet when I studied her in the mirror I knew something was wrong. My immediate reaction was that I was looking at a little girl in a grown-up black dress. The severity of the dress

All my clothes make me feel different. One of my little-girl outfits makes me feel like I am going to have fun all day. My flowery dress with the flowery top makes me feel sophisticated and like I am going to get a lot done. When I wear my red accessories I feel bold, and I want to go out and talk to people. I still choose my clothes the night before, but I do it by deciding what kind of day I want to have tomorrow.

Holly

communicated no part of Janice's essence. It was sexy, but it was dramatic in a way that Janice was not. Janice loved the outdoors, moved as if she was about to break into a run, and had soft coloring and sparkly blue eyes. I told her I felt it flattered her shape but it didn't suit her spirit. She was reluctant to agree. "Maybe this is what he wants," she said. "I want him to think I am a knockout, I want him to be impressed. But where would I wear it again? It isn't really me. But maybe it's worth it just for tonight. Oh, I don't know what to do!"

I can tell when a good crisis is brewing. I insisted we put the dress on hold, stop for coffee, and continue to look further. As we sat sipping our coffee, tears came to Janice's eyes. "I really want him to like me for me," she said, "but what if he doesn't?" The tears spilled over as Janice faced the pain of this age-old conflict.

Janice dried her eyes and we continued shopping. At our next stop we found a soft, slim jersey dress in a warm turquoise color. It gently clung to Janice's body, and the swing of the skirt suited her bounce and athletic energy. The bright blue of her eyes shined, and I could imagine her feeling comfortable and at home anywhere in this dress. I was delighted. She was so appealing, I knew if I met this lady at a party I would immediately feel drawn to her lightness and bouyancy. How different an impression it made from the black dress! But Janice was not fully convinced. "Is it really stylish? Will he like it?" What she really meant was, "Will it make me beautiful enough to capture and bewitch him?" I told her she would have to trust me that it was the perfect dress, and take her chances.

From what she told me later, all went well. "The real joy," she said, "came from being myself."

When we put our true essence out for all the world to see, we leave ourselves open to the risk that there will be no takers. Fortunately, most of us have discovered the reverse to be true. The truer we are to ourselves, the more like-minded people we attract. However, our society's emphasis on a specific "beauty" standard feeds the fear that we are not acceptable just as we are. We hunger for reassurance. When someone finds you attractive, that person becomes a mirror that allows you to see yourself reflected in admiring eyes. That admiration causes you to take notice of some of your own special qualities, and you find yourself feeling newly beautiful. It is only natural to want to please others, to be found attractive and desirable. But believing that you are beautiful should not be subject to the whims of others; it must be a reservoir of sureness that develops from deep within you.

The more certain you grow that your individuality is worth appreciating, the more comfortable you will become in expressing your beauty. The egocentric obsession with appearance we all find so offensive is simply an indication of a lack of self-love. The seemingly "vain" individual must prove herself at every turn, because she doesn't trust in her own beauty. Feeling beautiful can become as comfortable and natural as a soft flannel shirt. It does not become less important, merely less obsessive.

At a recent reunion, I ran into an old friend who greeted me by saying,"You look great! You're so 'out there.' " I smiled my thanks, although I was not sure exactly what she meant. Later in the evening she asked, "Don't you feel uncomfortable when people look at you? I often think I should try to look less noticeable to avoid the attention." Sarah was indeed quite striking, with black hair, milky pale skin, aqua eyes, and dramatic arching eyebrows. Even after I had done her colors, I noticed that she gravitated toward the most neutral of hues. Her dilemma brings up an important point. Coming into a fuller expression of beauty does not mean you will be besieged by attention. Until she mentioned it, I had no awareness of anyone "checking me out." I rarely notice glances, admiring or otherwise, because I am not looking for them to affirm my attractiveness. The time I care most about my appearance is when I am looking in my mirror at home. When I see my good points reflected, I can go on to whatever I am doing

The bottom line is self-love, and if you love yourself you will treat yourself in a way that expresses self-love. It is expressed in many different ways—how we treat ourselves as human beings and the people we attract around us. It is always the mirror image; we attract who we are, and we send out who we are.
Serita

with the confidence of knowing I look my best. After that satisfying moment in front of the mirror, I don't think about how I look. I forget my appearance and involve myself in the activities around me. I enjoy compliments, but I am not looking to see if I cause a stir. It no longer occurs to me to look and see if I am the thinnest (or fattest) person in the room, the best dressed, or the most handsomely escorted. When you believe in the beauty of your spirit, there is no reason to look to the outside for reassurance.

Sarah worried about calling attention to herself. My response to her, and to all the lovely women of the world, is "Why diminish any aspect of yourself?" You would not dim your intelligence, your strength, or your courage. How you look is a reflection of the inner you. Why compromise that? Your beauty is yours to celebrate, to share and, most importantly, to enjoy.

Growing confident in your appearance is all part of the process of evolution. My clients have told me that liking what they see in the mirror becomes surprisingly comfortable and natural. One lovely woman who had not felt happy with her reflection in many years described the feeling by saying, "I remember you. Welcome back!" In most cases, we feel fine about our appearance until something (or someone) convinces us otherwise. That inner reservoir of self-confidence may just be waiting to be awakened.

Once you change the downward spiral of negative experiences into a cycle of positive reinforcement, you will take increasing pleasure in your appearance. Success breeds success, and as you follow the suggestions in this book, your ability to build a wardrobe you feel satisfied with will improve. The newfound expression you experience through your clothing will allow you to discover more about yourself. The clothing you choose will contribute to how you feel, and how you feel will, in turn, contribute to the clothing you choose. The pattern will begin to spiral up instead of down.

When I look in the mirror now I feel like smiling at myself. When I leave for work in the morning, I look in the mirror and say, "Hey, I look terrific!" I have every right to give myself a compliment.

Gloria

The positive feelings gained from Clothing Your Spirit often last longer than the garments themselves. Stephanie's story presents a poignant example. With her children grown and away at college, Stephanie decided to take the adventuresome step of selling her house and embarking on a solo journey to Europe. She contacted me to help her plan a wardrobe that would take her from late summer into the winter. We created a wonderful ensemble from the ground up, and packed it into new, bright-red suitcases. When I took Stephanie's "before and after" photographs, the face that glowed back at me was shining and full of promise. Soon after her departure, I received a postcard full of the people she had met and the marvelous comments she had received about her clothes.

A month later a heartbreaking letter arrived. Her suitcases, and all their contents, had been stolen. Stephanie advised me to "brace yourself for another round of shopping" upon her return. "After enjoying the wonderful wholeness and confidence I experienced in the clothes," she wrote, "I know I won't be able to stand wearing my old things."

When Stephanie and I next met, following her return to San Francisco, I expected to find her down and dispirited at the prospect of starting over. Quite the opposite was true. "You know," she said, "I don't have things to wear that I like, but I feel okay. I have a sense of 'me.' I feel like a beautiful person in imperfect clothes."

Feeling beautiful goes far deeper than the inch of excess you try to work off at your aerobics class. You may feel the need to fight off the forces of aging, but without the passing of time, the marvelous process of evolution could not take place. Relish your beauty instead of fearing its loss. Look forward to the growing insights you will be able to express. Every phase of life offers its own rewards. Being pleased with yourself now is all you have today.

Life's difficulties treat us in ways that are not always beautifying. If stress manifests itself in weight gain, tell yourself you are now ripe and luscious. It works far better than condemning yourself as a fat and ugly failure. If you know you can look great even if you are above your ideal weight, you will avoid the panic that often results in continued overeating. Use the enjoyment and expression of your beauty to help you through trying times. Spending a little extra time on your lovely and familiar face can be comforting and consoling. Handle yourself gently. Keep doing the positive things that work for you.

Focus on what you like about yourself instead of what you don't. When you stop putting all your attention on areas you are less than happy with, their importance will magically diminish. Believing you have assets worth flattering is the first step to take towards allowing yourself to meet with your own approval. You do not have to continuously talk yourself into liking how you look. The clothes you are going to choose will help you do that. You can see the simple truth evident in the photographs. When someone dresses more in harmony with who she is, she looks better. It cannot help but make an impact on how you perceive yourself.

Until you feel yourself to be beautiful, the quest to improve your appearance will continue to take a great deal of your time. When I talked to the women featured in this book two years after their original interviews, I saw and heard a level of acceptance and appreciation I was not expecting. They told me every aspect of their appearance, from coordinating their wardrobe to worrying about their body, took less effort. These women were able to let go of their all-consuming concern with their appearance by delving in and accomplishing their long-held goal of looking beautiful. Only then could they allow caring for their appearance to become a relaxed and natural part of their lives.

When you Clothe Your Spirit, there is much to look forward to. You will look and feel better and better. Your wardrobe will be tailored to your individual needs, so you will have a suitable outfit for every occasion. Your money will go farther than ever before, because when you buy only things you love you feel less compelled to replace them as frequently. You will find yourself enjoying many of your clothes from one year to the next. A season may arrive and find you unable to purchase a new wardrobe in the latest style; when you discover you no longer feel deprived because of it, you will know you have arrived. From now on, you will be carrying your own unique sense of style around with you.

Creating a wardrobe you are happy with is a continuous undertaking. It involves a willingness to be open, to change, to re-evaluate, and to persevere. It is not always easy, but the rewards are great. Follow the suggestions you feel the most comfortable with until you are ready to give the others a try. Don't be too hard on yourself if you wear something too tight or buy something that's all wrong. Old patterns die hard, and there is intense social pressure helping them stay in place. Continue to return to the solutions that allow you to feel satisfied and successful.

The process of Clothing Your Spirit will help you to develop an unshakeable faith in the value of your uniqueness. Being "beautiful" is simply having enough confidence to think and act as if you are. There may be many glamorous magazines and videos leading you to believe otherwise, but the truth is all beauty originates within. Attractiveness radiates from the humor, intelligence, or happiness evident in a person's face. An expressionless face, no matter how perfect the features, is not pretty. How you appear on the outside IS a reflection of all that you are inside. There is no one you must please until you please yourself. Allow Clothing Your Spirit to become a personal and joyful project. One of life's greatest fulfillments is expressing all that you are and anticipating the wonder of all that you will become.

Clothing my Spirit was the catalyst that got me started in other areas of my life that needed some improvement. I began exploring my inner self, through groups and books. The clothes started all that, because they started me feeling good about myself. My outer appearance was okay, and that was how I was going to face the world. That gave me enough confidence to start facing the inner me.

Gloria

Acknowledgements

The hardest part of writing a book is believing you can do it. I had my doubts until the day I finished the final chapter. Without the encouragement of my wonderful friends and family, I never would have seen Clothe Your Spirit to completion.

My husband Jerry's faith and commitment never wavered. When I hesitantly told him I wanted to write a book, he gestured around the bookstore we were in at the time and said, "Of course you can write a book! If all those people wrote books, you can do it too." Over the two years it took me to complete Clothe Your Spirit, he never changed his tune.

I am grateful to my mother Lois Robin and to my father and stepmother Leonard and Connie Robin, for all the years of loving support that helped me develop the confidence necessary to embrace new challenges. They encouraged me to follow my passions, no matter what direction they might lead.

To my wonderful friends Deb Tweddell and Marilyn Curtis, my stepdaughter Sharon Freeman, and my brother Dan: thanks. Being there for me really made a difference.

For their sincere interest and for providing the great fashions that make my job so much easier, thanks to everyone at the clothing store Susan Matthews. For helping me look my best, a big thank you to designer Brian Fedorow for his stunning ensembles.

I would also like to thank the fantastic staff of At The Top salon. I couldn't have a better place to work or a nicer group of people to work with.

The vision of my publisher Christy Polk made Clothe Your Spirit a reality. Every author should be as lucky as I was to have such a wonderfully talented and upbeat person to work with.

Designer Kathleen Jaeger helped to make Clothe Your Spirit even better than I had imagined. Her creativity and hard work were very much appreciated.

Finally, I would like to thank all my clients for being so beautiful, expressive, and inspiring. Without you, the Clothe Your Spirit concept never would have been created. A special thank you to Holly, Debbie, Gloria, and Serita for giving so generously of their time and enthusiasm.

Loie's clothes from Susan Mathews
Debbie's clothes designed by Brian Federow.